STEPHEN KING
Not Just Horror

By Hans-Åke Lilja

BearManor Media.com

Typesetting and layout by PKJ Passion Global

Published in the USA by
BearManor Media
1317 Edgewater Dr #110
Orlando FL 32804
www.BearManorMedia.com

Softcover Edition
ISBN-10:
ISBN-13: 979-8-88771-367-0

Published in the USA by Bear Manor Media

Contents

Preface

For a number of years, Hans-Åke Lilja has devoted himself to a popular education project: to travel around Sweden lecturing about Stephen King, partly in order to convert those readers whose first reaction to a King novel is, "No way, I'll never read that scary awful stuff."

As this book will show you, there are many other aspects of King than that of the "horror guy", which means that everyone could find things to like in his work. To me, what I retain from his books is primarily his phenomenal depictions of *friendship,* particularly between younger and older characters. Certainly King is adept at showing us horror, but I consider his friendships to be his finest accomplishment.

What Hans-Åke knows about King verges on the horrifyingly thorough, and in this book he tells us about tales, short stories and unfinished novels I have never heard of. I find it a joy to have my knowledge of a favorite subject extended in this fashion. The many both funny and interesting anecdotes made me read the book quickly, almost in a single sitting.

Additionally, it contains two interviews Hans-Åke has conducted with King. My own experiences have taught me how much more satisfying it is to be interviewed by someone who has actually read some of what I have written. Hans-Åke has read *everything* by his interview subject, and you can tell how relaxed and talkative King becomes when he finds the interviews fun. This is a further accomplishment of this book.

But now I'll stop keeping you from exploring the multifaceted world of Stephen King, guided by the firm and knowledgeable grip of Hans-Åke Lilja. This is a book written by a sublime geek, in all the best meanings of the word. You will have fun.

John Ajvide Lindqvist

Introduction: Not Just Horror

Stephen King is often mentioned in connection with horror. Stephen King – the King of Horror, or Master of Horror are epithets used to market his books or the films made from his stories. Perhaps you wonder why this should be a problem. After all, he has written novels like *It* (Viking, 1986), *Pet Sematary* (Doubleday, 1983) and other scary stories. But though there is nothing wrong in calling him a masterful horror writer, he is many more things than that. And has written much which is not at all horror fiction, a fact unfortunately unknown to many.

Personally, I have been reading Stephen King's fiction for forty years. I have maintained a web page dedicated to his work for close to thirty years, am active on numerous Internet forums dedicated to him, have lectured on him for many years, published books on him and his work and consider myself an expert on his writings. On lecture tours I constantly meet persons who have never heard of Stephen King writing anything else than horror. Before I begin my talks, a handful of those in the audience almost always step up, some of them even librarians, to tell me that they are excited to learn a little about Stephen King. After which they add, "I haven't read many of his books, they are much too scary for me," or, even worse, "I haven't read anything by him, I've only seen a movie and it was much too gruesome." I always thank these people for coming to hear me talk about King even though they actually don't like his work. Then I tell them that he has written many stories which aren't in the least horrifying. "Really? Which ones?", they ask doubtfully, almost as if I were trying to trick them into reading something horrifying. But the fact is that Stephen King has written crime novels, psychological novels, wild west, science fiction, a musical and even a children's book. What I hope to do in my lecture, and the challenge I face, is to make just those skeptical readers want to in spite of their reservations at least try a Stephen King novel. And I honestly believe that I've fairly often succeeded.

The film titles I most often mention, primarily because I know that most people will recognize them, are *The Green Mile* (1999), *The Shawshank Redemption* (1994), and *Stand by Me* (1986), and invariably someone in the audience will ask, "Did *he* really write those? I've never heard that."

But he did. Not the film scripts, but the stories on which the films were based. If you know King's work, this is hardly as surprising as some people think, but it is perhaps understandable since the film companies in these particular cases have refrained from featuring Stephen King's name on their posters, since they assume that doing so would make potential viewers assume that the film is what they expect from him: a horror movie. Consequently on these films the author's name is printed in small type in the credits listed at the bottom of the poster, which hardly anyone bothers to read. All in order for the mainstream movie goer not to notice Stephen King's name and concluding something on the order of, "I don't feel like a horror movie, let's watch something else."

Why then is Stephen King so intimately associated with horror? The reason is obvious. Horror fiction was popular when King began to be published in the 1970s. His first novels, *Carrie* (Doubleday, 1974), *'Salem's Lot* (Doubleday, 1975) and *The Shining* (Doubleday, 1977), were all horror. In his afterword to his novella collection *Different Seasons* (Viking, 1982), King writes that his then editor, Bill Thompson, had warned him when he told Thompson about *The Shining.* "First the telekinetic girl, then the vampires, now the haunted hotel and the telepathic kid. You're gonna get typed." King had replied, "That's okay Bill. I'll be a horror writer if that's what people want. That's just fine." And initially it didn't bother King to be called a horror author, but as he developed as a writer, he also widened his repertoire to include other both genres and motifs. Despite that, he has been unable to shake off the horror stamp. And he was certainly not helped by early in his career both repeating

Robert Bloch's quip, "I have the heart of a small boy, it's in a jar on my desk", and making statements as, "I recognize terror as the finest emotion and so I will try to terrorize the reader. But if I find that I cannot terrify, I will try to horrify, and if I find that I cannot horrify, I'll go for the gross-out. I'm not proud." Quotes like these certainly didn't make readers view him less as a horror writer.

So what does today's Stephen King feel about being viewed as the premier horror writer in the world? In most interviews over many years he has expressed his dislike of being pegged in some specific field, since this may make many bypass his books and the films made from them without giving them a fair chance. It also means that many will never notice that King actually does many other things than just write horror. It is these things I intend to take a closer look at in this book.

And speaking of the book you are holding right now – perhaps while still in a store, trying to decide whether it's something to buy, or perhaps already at home and just beginning to read – you should know that it is all about Stephen King outside of his role as a master of horror. I have written it in order to give you a chance to discover the other side of King. The side which is not horror but something else, or rather several different other things. I will tell you about Stephen King the "actor" (and you will learn why I put quotation marks around the word), King the musician and King the children's book writer. Among other things. I also include the two telephone interviews I have conducted with him. Talking to him on the phone made me feel both enormously excited and just as enormously nervous, but I will tell you more about it further on.

I have read Stephen King since I was 13 years old, when my parents gave me a copy of *Carrie* for Christmas. He has been a constant presence for 40 years, entertaining me, surprising me and frightening me. So I dare claim that I know what I am talking about. And now I hope you will let me introduce you to an aspect of Stephen King not everyone is aware of, but despite this an aspect well worth exploring. Will you come along? Fine, take my hand, and we're off.

The Collaborator

When you think of authors, the first thing you'll consider probably isn't the stories they may have co-written with others. But there is a Stephen King persona who has cooperated with several other writers. The most famous of them was probably the now late Peter Straub, together with whom King wrote *The Talisman* (Viking, 1984) and *Black House* (Random House, 2001). But although this was King's most well-known cooperative venture, it was not by far the first time he worked together with another writer. The very first time was in fact already in 1960, when he and his childhood friend Chris Chelsey published a short story collection, printed on King's brothers small printing press and handbound. The brief volume was titles *People, Places & Things, volume 1*, and was published by what they chose to call Triad Publishing. Around 10 copies were printed, and of those a single copy is still known to exist, owned by King himself. The stories collected in the little booklet were:

- "The Hotel at the End of the Road" - Stephen King
- "Genius" - Chris Chelsey
- "Top Forty News, Weather, and Sports" - Chris Chelsey
- "Bloody Child" - Chris Chelsey
- "The Dimension Warp" - Stephen King
- "I've Got to Get Away!" - Stephen King
- "The Thing at the Bottom of the Well" - Stephen King
- "Reward" - Chris Chelsey
- "The Stranger" - Stephen King
- "A Most Unusual Thing" - Chris Chelsey
- "Gone" - Chris Chelsey
- "They've Come" - Chris Chelsey
- "I'm Falling" - Stephen King

- ”The Cursed Expedition” - Stephen King
- “The Other Side of the Fog” - Stephen King
- ”Scared” - Chris Chelsey
- “Curiosity Kills the Cat” - Chris Chelsey
- “Never Look Behind You” - Stephen King & Chris Chelsey

Eight of the 18 stories were written by King, ten by Chris Chelsey, and ”Never Look Behind You” the two friends wrote in collaboration.

”Never Look Behind You” is half a page long and tells of how George Jacobs, not a particularly nice person, is killed by an old woman in torn clothes because – as you might guess – he never looked behind him. I suspect that nobody will view this story as a masterpiece; it was a very short tale written by two 13-year-old boys wanting to be writers. Short, to the point, and entirely without any development.

Of the 18 stories in this first ”collection”, only two have been republished later. “The Hotel at the End of the Road” was to be reprinted by *Flip Magazine* in 1986, but it was folded before the story was published and another seven years passed before the story finally appeared in *Market Guide for Young Readers*, published by Writer's Digest Books in 1993. While ”I've Got to Get Away!” was printed in *Famous Monsters of Filmland* magazine number 202, 1994, but rewritten and retitled ”The Killer”. The story was originally told from the protagonist's point of view, but the rewritten version instead uses a third-person perspective.

Stephen King next collaboration was considerably more extensive. This time his collaborator was Peter Straub, whom we have already mentioned. Their friendship began after King had praised Straub's novel *Julia* (Coward, McCann & Geoghegan, 1975) and Straub had reciprocated by calling *The Shining* a masterpiece. Shortly after this, the King family was invited for dinner at the Straubs, and the idea of a collaboration began to take root. The fact that the two authors were quite different – Straub was influenced by both his mainstream literary background and his ten years in Dublin, Ireland, and in London, while Stephen King was inspired by genre fiction and current American events – if anything strengthened their wish to collaborate. After the decision was finally made, the story of 12-years old Jack Sawyer and his quest to save his dying mother by finding a talisman in the magical world of the 'Territories' began to take form. King wrote at his home in Bangor, Maine while Peter Straub wrote at his in Westport, Connecticut. They exchanged texts digitally, which was much harder in the early 1980s than it is now: they used telephone modems to call each other up and send their texts. Sometimes they also met physically and continued writing, taking turns at the computer. There was no clear distinction as to who wrote what in the final book; each author wrote until he ran out of ideas, then let the other take over. Some people have speculated that one of the collaborators wrote that part of the story which is set in the Territories, while the other wrote the parts set in our world, but this is incorrect. Both wrote scenes set in both the two worlds.

The Talisman was published in the United States on November 8, 1984, but though it started out high on the bestseller lists (and stayed there for quite a while), critics were far from satisfied. They did not view King and Straub, though both separately accomplished writers, to make for an ideal collaboration, and felt that the novel was much too slow. Stephen King has said that the reviews were "the worst I've ever gotten".

Movie rights to *The Talisman* were bought by Steven Spielberg already in 1982, two years before the book was published, and in an interview published in *Entertainment Weekly* in 2018, Spielberg explained the current situation:

"Universal bought the book for me, so it wasn't optioned. It was an outright sale of the book. I've owned the book since '82, and I'm hoping to get this movie made in the next couple of years. I'm not committing to the project as a director, I'm just saying that it's something that I've wanted to see come to theaters for the last 35 years."

Spielberg has more than once been on the verge of making his film version of *The Talisman*, but so far nothing has come off these efforts, despite 41 years now having passed since he initially bought the rights to the book and by now five years since he made the above statement. Currently, Netflix has announced its interest in producing a TV series from the book, and has hired brothers Matt and Ross Duffer, who wrote, produced and directed the *Stranger Things* series (five seasons, 2016–2024), to turn the novel into a further series. Should this become a reality, chances are that *The Talisman* will end up on the small screen within a year or two.

So far, Stephen King and Steven Spielberg have never collaborated on any project, but more than once been close to doing so. The first time was when Spielberg was set to film *Poltergeist* (1982) and wanted King's input on the film script. That time, Spielberg never managed to get in contact with King, who said, "I was on a ship going across the Atlantic to England." When he at last learned that Spielberg had tried to contact him, Spielberg had already gone on to other alternatives.

In the mid-1990s, Spielberg and King discussed creating a haunted house story, set in an old Victorian mansion, but got nowhere on the plot. A few years later Stephen King revisited the notion, and this time wrote *Rose Red* (2002) as a miniseries for ABC, based on the initial idea he and Spielberg had shared.

17 years after *The Talisman*, King and Straub published its sequel, *Black House*. The novel was off to a difficult start, being released on September 15, 2001, only four days after the 9/11 terrorist attack. Fantasy novels was the last thing most people thought about just then. And later, when the book was read, many – myself included – were surprised by its many strong connections to Stephen King's *Dark Tower* series. Whether *The Talisman* was set in the *Dark Tower* "universe" or not had already been discussed, and now the authors confirmed the notion that it was. Some found this to their liking, but others felt that they would have preferred Jack's adventures to be free of the tower and all its ramifications.

The plan was for King and Straub to write three novels about Jack Sawyer. Both authors have stated that they had a clear notion of all three books, and that what kept them from writing them was mainly their difficulties in finding a time and place to sit down together and get all of the story down on paper. Every time they happened to be at the same place and were photographed together, rumors began circulating: now it would happen, now they will finally write the third book. These rumors were especially persistent in 2018, since that was 17 years since the publication of *Black House*, which had in turn appeared 17 years after *The Talisman*. But no third book appeared.

Peter Straub also expressed his uncertainty of being able to match King's writing speed, and since he died in 2022, chances for a third book in the series must reasonably be viewed as very slim, since that would entail King writing it alone. But when it comes to King, nothing is impossible.

In 2004, King collaborated with Stuart O'Nan to write *Faithful: Two Diehard Boston Red Sox Fans Chronicle the Historic 2004 Season* (Scribner, 2004). As the book title clearly states, both authors are baseball enthusiasts and in particular fans of the Red Sox team. That they chose to chronicle the 2004 season was very good timing: in that year, the Red Sox won the World Series for the first time since 1918, finally breaking an 85-years long losing streak.

King and O'Nan also co-wrote a short story, "A Face in the Crowd" (Scribner, 2012), published only as an eBook and as an audiobook, read by Craig Wasson. It tells of Dean Evers, an elderly widower who spends most of his time watching baseball on TV. One evening he sees someone he recognizes in the audience, someone long dead. Evers at first thinks himself mistaken, but night after night he recognizes more and more individuals in the audience, all of them persons he knew before they died. Finally he decides to visit the stadium, to check whether his old friends really are there. A decision that turns out to be disastrous.

That Stephen King is a devoted baseball fan is obvious, not just from the book and story he wrote with Stuart O'Nan, but also from his previous nostalgic baseball poem "Brooklyn August" (in his collection *Nightmares and Dreamscapes* (Viking, 1993), and from his novella *Blockade Billy* (Cemetery Dance, 2010). But baseball is so far a major sport in only a handful of countries, outside of the US primarily in Japan, South Korea, and Taiwan, and consequently *Faithful* is one of the Stephen King books that have been translated into the least number of languages.

In addition to his writer friends, several of the members of Stephen King's family are also writers, and he has collaborated with some of them as well. The first instance of this is a brief short story, written in 1978 and obviously for fun and in order to amuse the eldest of the King children, Naomi (born 1970) and Joe (born 1972). "The King Family and the Wicked Witch" was written by Stephen King, and in this instance the collaboration consisted of his children illustrating the story. One of the drawings shows daddy Steve having his nose replaced by a banana.

As the children grew older, both Joe and his little brother Owen (born 1977) began writing stories of their own. Joe's full name is Joseph Hillstrom King, but when he began submitting professionally in 1995, he also began signing his work "Joe Hill" in order to succeed solely on his own merits rather than because of his relation to his father. In this he succeeded and had not only published both several stories and his first books, but also received numerous awards, before his real identity was disclosed.

King and Hill have so far collaborated on two published stories. The first was "Throttle", published in *He Is Legend*, a tribute anthology of stories inspired by Richard Matheson (Gauntlet, 2009). The story by King and Hill is inspired by Matheson's famous "Duel" (1971, filmed the same year by Steven Spielberg). In Matheson's story and film script, a car driver is hunted by a truck; King and Hill instead let a gang of motorcyclists be pursued by the truck. A comic book version of "Throttle" was published in 2012.

Three years later, they wrote ”In the Tall Grass”, a story serialized in *Esquire* magazine's issues for June/July and August, 2012. In the story, two siblings stop to stretch their legs during a long drive. They suddenly hear a you boy crying for help from the field across the road. The grass is too high for them to be able to see the boy, but they hear him and understand that he is lost. When they walk out into the grass to help him, they soon realize that they too are lost, and find that whatever they do, they get further and further away from both each other and the road. The story was later filmed for Netflix, directed by Vincenzo Natali, in 2019.

With his other son, Owen King, Stephen King has collaborated on a novel: *Sleeping Beauties* (Scribner, 2017), a book that has split King's readers into two camps: those who feel that the different writing styles of Stephen and Owen have combined into an interesting new voice, and those who simply don't care for it. The basic question in the novel is what would happen if all women in the world suddenly fell asleep. As the back cover text on the American mass market paperback says, ”In a future so real and near it might be now, a mysterious pandemic is causing women everywhere to suddenly go to sleep, shrouded in a cocoon-like gauze. Any attempt to awaken them is met with a reaction of feral, spectacular violence.”

The paperback was published in 2018, the year before the Covid pandemic shut down the world. In 2020, comic book version of the book was published, and AMC has bought the TV serial rights to the novel.

Apart from the mentioned King collaborations with his two sons, there are at least two further which very few people have ever read: ”But Only Darkness Loves Me”, by King and Joe Hill, and ”I Hate Mondays”, by Stephen and Owen King. These two are unfinished and have never been published, but are available in the Special Collection in the Raymond H. Fogler Library at the University of Maine. To read them, you must have permission and can only read the manuscripts in the library, not borrow or copy them.

One of those who has read both manuscripts was the late Rocky Wood, who in the course of a 17 days long research trip read numerous unpublished works at the Fogler Library. In his book *Stephen King: Uncollected, Unpublished* (Overlook Connection Press, 2012), he describes the story in "But Only Darkness Loves Me": "A boy is talking to a beautiful girl in a bar in Ledge Cove, Maine. She is too beautiful to look at directly, except in quick glances. She invites him back to her hotel but he only agrees to go to the lobby, not her room."

Only two pages remain of the story, and there is no information on when it was written. In the case of "I Hate Mondays", however, the entire story exists. Its five manuscript pages are clearly the work of a child and the story was almost certainly written for fun. It is undated, but Rocky Wood describes the plot: "Spike's wife has been kidnapped and is being held because she holds the combination to a bank's safe. The goons capture Spike by telling him they are holding her. Spike and Rita escape, killing most of the bad guys but in the process Rita is also killed. Finally, Spike kills the ringleader: 'And that was that'."

Neither of these stories can be called a masterpiece, and it is highly unlikely that we'll ever get the chance to read them in some future collection. Possibly King himself, Joe or Owen find inspiration in them for some future story or novel, but if so that will be the closest most of us will come to reading either of them. Unless we pay a visit to the Raymond H. Fogler Library.

A definitely more odd collaboration consists of the musical *Ghost Brothers in Darkland County*, which Stephen King wrote with John Mellancamp. Few people would associate King with musicals, but in fact he has tried his hand at this as well. According to King, what would in the end become *Ghost Brothers in Darkland County* started with a phone call from Mellancamp sometime around the turn of the century. He talked about an idea that had occurred to him, based on a true event in Indiana decades earlier. In a small cabin, two brothers had started arguing about a girl, and the quarrel ended with one of them killing the other, then setting off with the girl to drive back to the city but end up in a car crash that killed them both.

King liked the story and together he and Mellancamp began developing the incident into a full-length musical. But it took time. Gossip about the project began on the Internet around mid-2001, but the musical wasn't finished until eleven years later. It finally premiered at the Alliance Theater in Atlanta on April 11, 2012. By then the two-man team of King and Mellancamp had been enlarged with T. Bone Burnett, who directed the musical. Burnett also played a major hand in casting and recording the *Ghost Brothers in Darkland County* album. The first character to be cast was "The Shape", and Burnett immediately knew who he wanted for that part: "Elvis Costello's name came up. Who could be better playing the Devil?"

The story is set in the small town of Lake Belle Reve in Mississippi and is focused on two pairs of brothers: the ghosts Jack and Andy, who have died in a murder and suicide, and their nephews, the living Frank and Drake, who seem to be on course for the same fate that met their uncles. Joe, younger brother of Jack and Andy and the father of Frank and Drake has decided that it's time to divulge his own horrible secret and intends to do it in the place where his two brothers met their tragic fate. In his introduction to the book version of the musical, Stephen King writes: "Joe gets his family to come out to the old family cabin by the lake, not knowing that the ghosts from that old tragedy are still there. The fun of the story is watching the father tell his sons this story that he's held for so long and seeing how the ghosts react to it."

And John Mellencamp disclosed how he and King worked: "Steve would call me up and go, 'We need a song like this to fill this place'. I really hate writing songs about myself, so to be able to go 'OK, now you're a ten-year-old boy, what would he say? Now you're a 19-year-old girl trying to attract the attention of a barroom of fellas'…that was just fun to do."

In June, 2013, the musical was also released as a book and on CD, and now very famous artists were involved. Kris Kristofferson, Meg Ryan, Roseanne Cash, Elvis Costello, Matthew McConaughey and Sheryl Crow were some of them. All both had spoken lines and sang. But unfortunately they never performed the musical on stage. The book version was also released as an eBook, with added videos and soundtracks, so that you as you read you can also hear the songs and spoken lines. This is by far the best way of appreciating the musical, at least for those who never get the chance to see it live. So far, it has been performed only in the United States, but hopefully there will be a world tour at some future date.

Stephen King's latest collaboration was with author and Cemetery Dance publisher Richard Chizmar. Together they have written the Gwendy Peterson trilogy. She starts out as an inhabitant of Castle Rock, Stephen King's fictional Maine town, and in the first and shortest of the books, *Gwendy's Button Box* (Cemetery Dance, 2017) we meet Gwendy as a twelve-year-old in 1974, when she meets Richard Farris (who happens to have the same initials as another Stephen King character). Farris gives Gwendy responsibility for a box full of buttons and levers. The idea is that she must keep it safe from ending up in the wrong hands. In the second volume, Gwendy's Magic Feather (Cemetery Dance, 2019), written by Chizmar alone, Gwendy is 32 and has become a politician, when she again is visited by Farris. In the third and last volume, again co-written by King and Chizmar, Gwendy is 64 and a US Senator, but is given a final task to perform by Farris.

The trilogy began when King had started a story for which he could find no satisfying ending. He mailed it to fellow horror author Chizmar and suggested he might come up with something. Chizmar, did, added some text of his own and sent it back to King, who added more to it. They continued writing in this fashion until the book was done. King was unable to contribute to the second book, but returned as co-author for the third and last.

Just as in *Black House*, which King wrote with Peter Straub, the last of the Gwendy novels has numerous references to the *Dark Tower* series. But King and Chizmar also, as noted, take us back to Castle Rock, in which parts of novels like *The Dead Zone* (Viking, 1979), *Cujo* (Viking, 1981), *The Dark Half* (Viking, 1989) and *Lisey's Story* (Scribner, 2006) takes place.

It would be very surprising if we have seen the last story or novel King will co-write with others. But for the main part, he has always written alone. And perhaps that is how he does it best, for, as Peter Straub said, what other writer can actually keep up with Stephen King?

The Children's Book Author

Most people are surprised to learn that Stephen King has written a book for children. In truth, it is certainly a fairly unsettling children's book, but it is still intended for children. *Charlie the Choo Choo* (Simon & Schuster, 2016) is in fact taken from *The Waste Lands* (Donald M. Grant, 1991), the third book in King's seven-volume epic *The Dark Tower*, where *Charlie the Choo Choo* is a book which Jake Chambers, one of the novel's main characters, buys in a bookstore called The Manhattan Restaurant of the Mind, and which later comes to play a significant role in the novel. In Jake's world, the book is written by Beryl Evans, while in the world of Roland, the protagonist of all the Dark Tower books, it was written by Claudia y Inez Bachman, wife of the deceased Richard Bachman (and a Stephen King pen name).

For the marketing of the film *The Dark Tower* (2017) at Comic Con in San Diego, 150 copies of *Charlie the Choo Choo* were printed, and at one of the merchandise tables at the convention was actress Allison Davis, who in the role of Beryl Evans, the book's author, was signing them. This resulted in there being 150 copies of a book signed by the fictitious author of the book, which is in fact written by Stephen King under a pen name. Convoluted? Certainly, but fans loved it and some of the signed books were sold for very high prices on eBay during the weeks following Comic Con. To add extra spice to the comedy, the front of the book jacket carries a quote saying,

"If I were ever to write a children's book, it would be just like this! – Stephen King"

After Comic Con was over and the movie had premiered, a new edition was printed and sold at a normal price, so that anyone wanting a copy could buy one. I have no idea whether children actually like it, but why not try reading it to them if you have small kids?

The story is a fairly typical children's book. We meet engineer Bob who discovers that his train, Charlie, is actually alive. They become friends and are both devastated when Charlie is forced into retirement when replaced by a newer engine. But as you might guess, before the story ends Charlie becomes a hero and comes back into active service. The book illustrations are based on the cover, painted by Ned Dameron while preparing the cover for the fourth Dark Tower book.

In fact, the book is nowhere on view in the film it was supposed to help advertise, which is a pity. It would have been fun to see it at least appear as an "easter egg" (a hidden insider joke between an author or director and dedicated fans). It does, however, appear in another film adaptation based on a Stephen King novel. In the Apple TV+ serial of *Lisey's Story*, it is visible in a scene where a character visits a library.

Of course, *Charlie the Choo Choo* isn't Stephen King's only book for young readers. He initially wrote *Eyes of the Dragon* (Philtrum Press, 1984) for his daughter Naomi. He wrote the book in 1983 and next year published it under his own imprint, Philtrum Press, in a limited edition illustrated by Kennety R. Linkhauser. Not until 1987 was it published in a commercial edition by Viking. The Viking edition is also slightly different from the original Philtrum version, largely because an editor had now worked on the book, which had not earlier been the case.

The originally intended title for the book was "The Napkins". His daughter had shown no interest at all in reading King's work, and he therefore decided to write a fantasy novel, since that was the kind of fiction she liked. At first he never even intended to have it published, since it was something he wrote only for Naomi. On his official web page, stephenking.com, he talks about getting the idea for the book:

"Although I had written thirteen novels by the time my daughter had attained an equal number of years, she hadn't read any of them. She's made it clear that she loves me, but has very little interest in my vampires, Ghoulies, and slushy crawling things. I decided that if the mountain would not go to Mohammed, then Mohammed must go to the mountain.

I sat down one night in our western Maine house to start this story, then called *The Napkins*. Eventually the tale was told, and Naomi took hold of the finished manuscript with a marked lack of enthusiasm. That look gradually changed to one of rapt interest as the story kidnapped her. It was good to have her come to me later and give me a hug and tell me the only thing wrong with it was that she didn't want it to end."

It is obvious that *Eyes of the Dragon* is no typical Stephen King novel, and was written for a very different audience than his earlier work: it is a story more suited to be told by the campfire than to be read. The novel features a narrator who tells us the story, which gives it a feel much different from King's usual third person narration which makes us experience his stories firsthand. There are also passages in the book that seem written expressly to satisfy his young, critical daughter, who was its single intended reader. Sometimes you get the feeling that the King family itself is portrayed in some passages, where they seem to play minor parts in the story. In one scene, Prince Peter is playing with his mother's dollhouse, and the family living in the house is strikingly similar to the King family.

Additionally, many of the protagonists of *Eyes of the Dragon* are children, which is typical of stories intended for young readers. Throughout, it is children who see clearly how things really are, and which persons actually are mean. The meanest of all in the novel is Flagg, whom we recognize from many of Stephen King's stories, not least from the Dark Tower series and from *The Stand* (Doubleday, 1978). However, in *The Eyes of the Dragon* he is toned down to be a bit less evil and horrifying, or in other words adjusted for younger readers. The only thing in the book which to me feels less than a natural part of a story intended for young readers occurs early on, when we learn more of King Roland's background and in that context are informed that he is not particularly interested in sex. It doesn't bother me, nor do I believe that I am in any sense a prude, but it does feel as perhaps not appropriate for a 13-year-old reader. Or at least as not quite matching the rest of the book.

While both *The Eyes of the Dragon* and, if to a lesser extent, *Charlie the Choo Choo* are well-known King titles, his first story written for children isn't. "The King Family and the Wicked Witch" is dedicated to King's two eldest children, Naomi and Joe. It was published in *Flint*, August 25, 1977, but was probably written already in 1976, since in the story Naomi (born in 1970) is six while Joe (born in 1972) is four.

Reading "The King Family and the Wicked Witch" I can't help feeling that this was a story King told his children at bedtime, and wrote down to preserve for Naomi and Joe when they grew older. The story is about the wicked witch Hanzel and the King family, which consists of Naomi who is six and goes to school, Joe who is four and due to his age is in school only two days per week, a daddy who writes books and a mommy who writes poetry and cooks. Hazel the witch hates the King family for being the happiest family in Bridgton, and therefore tricks them into eating four magical cookies. The daddy gets a banana cookie, which instantly changes his nose into a banana and makes it impossible for him to write anything else than the word "banana". The mommy gets a milk bottle cookie, which changes her hands into milk bottles. Naomi and Joe get a crying cookie each and are unable to stop crying.

But of course the King family are the heroes of the story, and all ends well. The wicked witch begins farting and farts so explosively that she blows herself to the moon. When the story was published in the *Flint*, its editor warned parents from reading it if they were overly sensitive: "If some of you parents might be offended by the word "fart", you'd better not red it - but don't stop your kids, they'll love it!"

It is easy to find copies of *Charlie the Choo Choo* and *The Eyes of the Dragon*. It takes some effort to get hold of "The King Family and the Wicked Witch". But don't give up. Remember what *Flint*'s editor wrote – you'll "love it!"

The Publisher

In 1982, 1983 and 1985, Stephen King sent no Christmas cards to his friends. Instead he sent short, stapled books which contained parts of a story he called *The Plant*. The three segments he sent were the first three parts of an intended longer story, and to integrate it in his business and simplify the production process, King formed a small publishing company which he named Philtrum Press, and which was based in his office and handled primarily by his long-time assistant Marsha DeFilippo. "Philtrum" is the word for what is also called the "medial cleft", the vertical groove running from the nasal septum, which divides the two nostrils, to the middle of the upper lip. King has never commented on the origin of the name, nor on whether he used the word in its biological sense or just though it funny or interesting.

After the three initial parts of *The Plant*, King decided to let the story rest since in his opinion it began to feel too similar to the play and films *Little Shop of Horrors* (originally a 1960 film directed by Roger Corman from a script by Charles B. Griffith, then a 1982 rock musical written by Howard Ashman, finally a 1986 film version of the musical, directed by Frank Oz from a screenplay by Howard Ashman), and he had absolutely no wish to be sued for plagiarism. It would take all of fifteen years before those who were not on King's Christmas card list got a chance to read the story.

But the three instalments of *The Plant* were not the only Philtrum Press publications. Already in 1984, when no new part of the serial was published, Philtrum published a limited first edition of *The Eyes of the Dragon*, printed in 1,250 copies and signed by Stephen King. A thousand of those copies were sold, but three years passed before the book was issued commercially and made available in bookstores. King's initial idea, as discussed in the previous chapter, was to write the novel only for his daughter Naomi, and when he decided to publish it himself he wanted it to be a unique edition, and turned to a friend of his university days, Michael Alpert, who helped design the book. In the official Stephen King newsletter *Castle Rock*, Alpert commented, "I knew that I would not be bound by the usual constraints of commercial publishing but instead I would have the kind of opportunity that book-designers can usually only dream about."

The final book had a larger format than the most hardcover novels, was illustrated in black and white and was printed on a finer paper quality, imported from France and intended to feel as if the pages were made of soft fabric, as in napkins (which play an important part in the plot). Alpert worked on the book for over a year before being satisfied.

When King three years later agreed to have the novel published in a second edition by his trade publisher, a number of textual changes were made. For one thing, Deborah Brodie, the children's book editor at Viking, wanted the Ben Staad character to be introduced earlier in the story than in its original version, and King agreed to this. But the main reason for the changes to the text was that no editor had ever read through the manuscript before it was published by Philtrum Press.

After the three parts of *The Plant* and *The Eyes of the Dragon*, Philtrum Press fell dormant for a dozen years before its next book appeared: *Six Stories* (Philtrum Press, 1997) was a collection of stories written by King, and was again published in a limited edition of 1,100 copies, out of which 900 were sold. As a personal aside, I can mention that it was the first limited edition book I myself ever bought. The Internet had by then given also those not living in the United States a chance to secure copies of rare new books. *Six Stories* was originally sold for $80, but now commands prices from more than ten times that and up. The book contained "Lunch at the Gotham Cafe", "L.T.'s Theory of Pets", "Luckey Quarter", "Autopsy Room Four", "Blind Willie", and "The Man in the Black Suit", all of the stories printed for the first time, and this was frustrating to many avid Stephen King readers. But in 1999, a greatly revised version of "Blind Willie" was incorporated in the episodic novel *Hearts in Atlantis* (Scribner), and in 2002 the other five stories, a couple of them with minor revisions, were included in King's story collection *Everything's Eventual* (Scribner).

The next Philtrum Press book was released in 1999, as part of a celebration. On April 6, Stephen King gave a party at Tavern on the Green in New York to mark the 25th anniversary of his first book, *Carrie* (Doubleday, 1974). Over a hundred guests had been invited, and at each place was a small book entitled *The New Lieutenant's Rap*, published by Philtrum. The book was placed in an envelope adorned with peace stickers, and each recipient also got a necklace with a peace sign. Every guest also received a signed copy of the non-Philtrum book *The Girl Who Loved Tom Gordon* (Scribner, 1999) and four pages of in all 25 questions concerning King's books. The invitation to the party had read:

Dear many –

On April 4, 1974, Doubleday published my first novel,
Carrie, and provoked a nationwide storm of disinterest.
I preserved, however, and on April 6, 1999, I'm throwing
a party at Tavern on the Green in New York City to
celebrate my 25 years as a writer. I hope that you
and your significant other, or a close friend (they
are often but not always the same), will come and help
me. There will be lots of food and party favors and
amusing chatter. Dress is casual, bluejeans fine.
Please RSVP, using the card enclosed, to Julie Eugley.
Don't be a cockadoodie brat. Come to my party.

7:00 p.m.   *Steve King*

Philtrum Press had printed 500 copies of *The New Lieutenant's Rap*, which King had written by hand. When the party was over, between thirty and forty of the guests had left their copies in the restaurant, and those were thrown out when the restaurant staff cleaned up. The remaining copies were retained by King and have never been sold. The story itself was later completely revised and published as "Why We're in Vietnam", in King's episodic novel *Hearts in Atlantis* (Scribner, 1999).

In the year 2000, King made a new effort to publish *The Plant*. This time he did so in eBook format and sold directly from his home page. He also chose to change the story in order to make it less reminiscent of *Little Shop of Horrors*. In 2000, an eBook was very different from what it has become now. There were no electronic eBook readers; what constituted an eBook was simply a pdf file you could download and read on screen or as a printout. Each part of the novel was made available on King's home page, and anyone could easily download it. But there was one condition: each new monthly installment would be put up only if a minimum of 75 percent of those who had downloaded the previous one had paid one dollar for it. Payment consisted in sending a dollar bill via mail to a given address – this was also long before electronic payment services like PayPal existed.

King has said that the experiment was on the whole successful: "With no printing costs, publisher's cuts or agents' fees to pull it down, costs are low to the point of nonexistence, and the profit potential is unlimited." But King didn't finish the story this time either, and the sixth installment of the story, in December, 2000, became the last. In *Time* magazine, December 10, Stephen King wrote, "Do Parts 1 through 6 constitute an entire novel? In the sense that there's a beginning, a middle and a resolution, yes. Readers will be as satisfied as they would be with, say, the first volume of a trilogy like Philip Pullman's *His Dark Materials* (not that I am claiming the same literary quality; never think that). Right now I'm returning to print publishing because I love it and because I have a contract to fulfill--two books remaining."

He also stated that he intended to continue publishing *The Plant* during the Summer of 2001, but this never happened. Readers had gotten more of it than had previously been sent out as Christmas cards, but the final part was still missing. And is still missing 23 years later. King may of course still return to *The Plant* at some point, but I won't hold my breath. He seems to have moved on from it.

Stephen King has always been opposed to America's very liberal gun laws, and in 2013 Philtrum Press published his essay *Guns*, written after the Sandy Hook Elementary School in Newtown, Connecticut, mass shooting on December 14, 2012, when 20-year-old Adam Lanza killed 26 people, 20 of them six or seven years old children. In his essay, King details his reasons for letting his novel *Rage* (as by "Richard Bachman", Signet, 1977) and the version of *The Bachman Books* (New American Library, 1985) containing it, go out of print. *Guns* was issued as an eBook in January, and as an audiobook read by Christian Rummel, though from Audible Studios, not from Philtrum, in February. King's official website states that, "All profits from *Guns* will benefit the Brady Campaign to Prevent Gun Violence."

All Philtrum Press books so far discussed were written by Stephen King himself, but King the publisher has also made room for another author – in 1987, Philtrum published Don Robertson's novel *The Ideal, Genuine Man*.

Don Robertson, who died at 70 in 1999, was an author King had admired sine his youth, and who was a major influence on his writing. According to Robertson, he had read King's novel *Christine* (Viking, 1983) and discovered that some places in it had seemed to have been borrowed from his own books, so "I wrote him a note filled with mock outrage, threatening to sue him and a friendship ensued."

King read Robertson's unpublished *The Ideal, Genuine Man*, and according to Robertson thought that his story of a desperate, bigoted, and unwell retired truck driver whose wife is dying from cancer and who finally loses control and starts killing was the best novel since *War and Peace*. Philtrum Press published the book in a numbered, limited first hardcover printing of 500 copies signed by both King (who wrote the "forenote") and Robertson, and in a regular hardcover trade edition of 2,700 copies.

Kings ambition was never to let Philtrum Press grow into a publishing giant. Rather, the idea was for him to be able to publish whatever he felt like, when he felt like it. History has shown that he has stuck to this limited vision, and consequently it is impossible to guess what, if anything, King the Publisher will publish next.

The Promoter

In late 2013 Stephen King did something unusual: he went to Europe in order to promote his new novel, *Doctor Sleep* (Scribner, 2013). Previously he hade been in London in 2006 to promote *Lisey's Story* (Scribner, 2006), and before that also in London in 1998 to promote *Bag of Bones* (Scribner, 1998). As you can surmise, King doesn't habitually travel to Europe, so when he does visit, it is something of an event. And now it was time for one. King was to begin his visit in France, then go to Germany. Fans from all over Europe (including myself) bough flight tickets and booked hotel rooms. This was not to be missed.

King started his tour in France on November 12, then go on to Germany and return to the United States on November 20. For a signing in Paris, a hundred fans already waited in line twelve hours before King would arrive, and with a couple of hours still to go the line was almost up to five hundred admirers. Perhaps this doesn't sound very impressive if you think of the enormous lines of people wanting tickets to major rock concerts, but keep in mind that Stephen King is an author, and authors seldom attract, and that even if King managed to sign four book per minute during the two hours he was to spend in the bookstore, he would still not manage to sign five hundred books. In other words, the enthusiasts waiting at the end of the line had cause to be worried. King's official website later reported that more than 3,000 people attended the signing. If this was really the case, not all of them could possibly have left with a signed book.

On November 16, King made his last public appearance in France, giving a public reading at Le Grand Rex cinema and concert hall, then went on to Germany for another reading at the USO Warrior Center in Ramstein on November 18, then a "meet and greet" event in nearby Munich. On November 20, he was to give a press conference, a further reading and a final reception in Hamburg, before leaving for home. I had the privilege of attending the last two events.

For me, November 20th began with a two hour drive to the airport, then a little over an hour's flight and finally a further hour-long bus trip to central Hamburg. This was to be my second meeting with Stephen King, the first having been at a publisher's party in London. This time, King's German publisher Heyne had invited me to both the reading and the informal reception.

We had strict orders to be at Congress Center Hamburg no later than 6.30 PM. If we were late, we could not be guaranteed to meet Stephen King. Both I and everyone else came early. Nobody wanted to risk missing out. On arriving, everyone was given a bracelet to prove our right to attend, a ticket to the reading and a name tag to wear at the later reception. Then we waited. At exactly 6.30 we were escorted backstage where we would meet King in less than half an hour. While we waited we were offered snacks and drinks. A few had some, but most of those present were much too nervous to eat anything.

Then the time came. Tension in the room was almost palpable. People nervously looked in the direction where King would enter, or looked at each other with nervous smiles. Then he was suddenly there.

Stephen King knows how to handle his audiences. He calmly walked round to shake everyone's hand before heading for the table where he would sign our books. Since he ran a few minutes late, it was decided that he would just sign his name, not add any personal notes; that way, everyone present would be able to get a signed book.

Here, I must again stress how professionally King acts when meeting his readers. He not only signed quickly and efficiently, but also calmly and naturally shook everyone's hand again, took the time to exchange a few words and let all who wanted to take a photo. When my time came I handed him the copy of the German translation of *Doctor Sleep* I had decided to get signed. I had also brought a copy of the Swedish translation of *The Dark Tower VII: The Dark*

Tower (Scribner, 2004; the Swedish edition, called *Det mörka tornet*, was published by Bra Böcker in 2009), but since *Doctor Sleep* was the book he was in Germany to promote, I thought it the preferable alternative. King signed it, and when I asked for a photo, he said, "of course".

In advance, I had asked my friend Anders, who was my traveling companion, to be ready to take a picture. But at the same moment he did so, the photographer hired by King's publisher also took one, and the result was that King looked at him while I looked at Anders. Luckily I realized this and asked King for a second photo, one where we both looked at the same camera, and he agreed to this. It turned out to be a great picture. Then I shook his hand, thanked him for all his books (this too Anders managed to capture) and made place for the next person in line.

It went on in the same way until King said that he would soon have to leave and only had time to sign a very few books more. I realized that those now in line already had had one book signed and now were waiting to have another one. Since I, too, had brought a second book, I fetched my Swedish copy of *The Dark Tower* and placed it before King. He signed it, said, "Okay, that's it, thank you all", and left. The informal meeting was over. But it had been a more than memorable experience, and now we could look forward to his reading.

We were shown to our places, which turned out to be perfect – fifth row, right in front of the stage middle where King would be seated. Nothing could have been much better than that. The reading took one hour and forty-five minutes, and again I was struck by how natural King seems to be in situations like this. Those who believe that authors are geeks just huddling alone in their homes will have to think again. At least as far as King goes. He jokes, read from *Doctor Sleep*, talked about various things and replied to questions as if he had never done anything else. Much of what he said obviously was about *Doctor Sleep*, which after all was the reason for his being there, but he also told us about an idea that had come to him while he was stuck in a Paris traffic jam a few days earlier. The car he was in stopped for a red light and King looked into the car next to his. So close and yet so far away. The people in that car had no idea of him looking at them. He and they seemed to be in different universes in spite of being just a dozen feet from each other. Then King asked if we wanted to hear the idea he had gotten. The whole audience roared "YES!" and King went on:

"This is like pissing a good story out on the ground. Usually they're better if they just stay inside but I just love this concept."

And then he told us.

"So, here's this guy who flies into La Guardia airport and his plane is late and he goes down to get his luggage and his luggage is of course the last one off the plane and the thing is he's coming to New York because although he's married, he has a mistress and he told his wife he was going to be home tomorrow but he's been detained on business. So, he's all ready and gearing to go when he has all these things holding him back. So, the plane is late, luggage is last, he goes out to the taxi, he's at the end of the queue and he finally gets a cab, and he goes into New York. As the cab pulls up next to another car, he looks into it and sees a woman and a man sitting there and as he looks the man takes a razor out of his jacket and cuts the woman's throat. Well, what does this guy do now? I don't know…"

In its August 2014 issue, *Esquire* published Stephen King's story "That Bus Is Another World", and in 2015 it was included in his collection *The Bazaar of Bad Dreams* (Scribner, 2015). It is obvious that this is the story King told his audience about in Hamburg. When I read it felt very special to have been given a glimpse into its inception, and to simultaneously have been given some insight into how King works and how the ideas he gets are transformed into stories.

One of the other stories in *The Bazaar of Bad Dreams* is called "Bad Little Kid". That story as well is linked to King's visit to France and Germany. In early 2014 there began to be whispers about King preparing a gift for his fans in France and Germany, as a thank-you for the warm reception he had been given there in the previous year. In February it was disclosed that King had written "Bad Little Kid" and that the story would be published only in French and German. The short story was around forty pages long and would be released as an eBook on March 14. King's official web page explained why King had decided to publish his story in this fashion:

"Stephen's visit in Germany and France last November was not only for his fans a very special event, but also for him. To thank all his German and French fans for their warm welcome he came up with a great idea: He wrote a story, "Bad Little Kid", which will be available in eBook format from 14th of March just in German ("Böser kleiner Junge") and French ("Sale Gosse")."

Many fans who didn't understand French or German felt frustrated. There was suddenly a new Stephen King story which they were unable to read. However, a few months later it was revealed that the exclusive contract for publication only in French and German would run out in the Summer of 2015, and that the story would consequently be included in King's collection *The Bazaar of Bad Dreams*, which would be published that Fall. King's fans could heave a sigh of relief.

I, too, was one of those frustrated fans who disliked having to wait for the story. I even tried using software to digitalize the text and then use Google Translate on it, but neither the French or German version led to any enjoyable result. Nevertheless, in spite of my frustration I could still applaud King's gesture to his fans in France and Germany. During his visit, they truly showed him how greatly they appreciated him.

But just as Stephen King's name appeals, it can also deter. Some of the films made from his stories are good examples of this. For in spite of most people agreeing that King's books and stories are in most cases better than the films based on them, many of the films have been quite successful in cinemas. Despite the fact that most of them are inferior, and that you actually know this if you have already seen a number of them, there is something that makes huge audiences come to see a new Stephen King film. The 2017 remake of *It* was released in more than 4,000 theatres in the US, and grossed in excess of $100 million over its first weekend. Not all, but certainly many of those who went to see the movie did so because it was based on a Stephen King novel. They expected, and received, a horror story.

But sometimes, King's name is a liability rather than a draw. It is no secret that *The Shawshank Redemption* always ends up at the top of almost all favorite movie lists, but this hasn't always been the case. At its premiere in 1994, the film didn't even earn back its production costs, and this made it a failure. More people saw it in 1995, after it was nominated for seven Oscars including the one for best movie. But it won in none of its categories.

The stars of the film have their own theories about its lack of early popularity. In 2014, Morgan Freeman told *Vanity Fair* that the film's title was its main problem: "Because of the film's vague title, no one could accurately recommend it, even if they had seen it. Nobody could say *Shawshank Redemption*. Your friends say, Ah, man, I saw this movie, The ... what was it? *Shank, Sham, Shim*? Something like that. Anyways, terrific. Well, that doesn't sell you."

Tim Robbins, who played the film's other lead role, agreed in an interview with *Entertainment Weekly*: "And that makes sense too, because for years after that film came out, people would come up to me and say, You know, I really liked you in that film *Scrimshaw Reduction* or *Shimmy, Shimmy, Shake or Shankshaw* – you know, so many different ways that people got it wrong."

Today, the movie has had both the redress and the accolades it deserve, and most have even begun to learn its name. But regardless of whether it was or wasn't the film's title that led to its initial obscurity, it has never been marketed using King's name on its posters. And the reason for this is to avoid movie goers assuming that it is a horror movie. Anyone looking closely would of course see King's name in the credits given in small typeface at the bottom of the posters, but how many people read that? Instead, the names on top which everyone saw were those of the lead actors, Morgan Freeman and Tim Robbins. Many who've seen the film even refuse to believe that it is made from a Stephen King story. King himself has often told the story of his meeting with an elderly lady in a Florida shop: "I was in a supermarket down here in Florida, and I came around the corner and there was a woman coming the other way. She pointed at me, she said, I know who you are! You're Stephen King! You write all of those horrible things. And that's okay. That's alright. But I like uplifting things, like that movie *Shawshank Redemption*. And I said, I wrote that! And she said, No you didn't. No you didn't."

The Shawshank Redemption isn't the only film that has been marketed without King's name being used. None of the posters for *The Green Mile*, *Stand by Me* or *Dolores Claiborne* feature him as author. When I lecture on King, there is usually at least someone in the audience who has seen one of these three films without realizing that it is based on Stephen King's work. This is perhaps particularly the case with *The Green Mile*, where marketing focus has been centered on the lead role played by Tom Hanks.

In spite of the above, please let me clarify that what I say here is hardly any great revelation. None of the film producers involved have worked hard at hiding Stephen King's involvement with the films mentioned, they simply refrain from trumpeting it. If you are a Stephen King fan, or if you pay attention to the posters or trailers for the films, you will certainly see King's name. What the companies have wanted to avoid was that spontaneous movie goers avoid these films because they assume them to be horror movies when in fact they definitely are not. That this could work is probably easier to understand when you realize that all of these movies were made before Internet was suddenly in every man's and woman's pocket. Rob Reiner's *Stand by Me* premiered in 1986, Frank Darabont's *The Shawshank Redemption* in 1994, Taylor Hackford's *Dolores Claiborne* in 1995 and Frank Darabont's *The Green Mile* in 1999. In those years, many would simply walk into a cinema and pick a movie to see, not seldom based on their posters. Things are very different today, when people sit at home, look for information and reviews and perhaps watch trailers before they make up their minds. But the fact remains: while King's name is a selling point for horror movies, it has the opposite effect for films belonging to other categories. And what this also shows, of course, is that very many people view Stephen King as synonymous with horror.

The Actor

There is a rumor going that claims that Stephen King is onscreen in all films made from his stories. Let's dismiss that one here, once and for all. If you consider the fact that more than a hundred feature films have been made from his stories, you should quickly realize that if that claim was true, King would hardly have the time to write any new books at all. But the notion is appealing, and people like to believe in appealing things. Alfred Hitchcock probably had the same problem. (No, he wasn't visible in all of the features he directed, but to be fair, he did make an appearance in forty of the fifty-three that are still around.)

It happens now and then when I give a talk on King that someone will ask whether he really appears in all of "his" films, and that I can see in his face (those who ask in this fashion are almost all male) that he simply won't listen when I try to explain that no, he really isn't in all those film. More than once I have been tempted to instead just say, "Of course, and wasn't he great in the remake of *Pet Sematary*?" In fact, King is not in that 2019 film, but I would love the feeling of knowing that the questioner would spend his entire evening checking through the film frame by frame to find King. But I haven't done so. Yet.

So far, King has made an appearance in 16 films based on his stories, in a handful not based on his own work, and in a few where he just is himself. He has also lent his voice to shows like *The Simpsons* and *Frasier*. His acting debut was in George A. Romero's *Knightriders* (1981), which is not based on anything by King. He and his wife Tabitha play a couple having a picknick while watching a mediaeval tournament. Both have speaking parts, and King delivers his dialog with his mouth full of food, commenting on the tight dresses of the players. It is a small but entertaining role. His single lead part is in that segment of *Creepshow* (1982) which is entitled "The Lonesome Death of Jordy Verrill", and King has the title role, playing the not too bright and out of luck Jordy Verrill, who sees a meteorite fall on his land. Verrill immediately starts thinking of making extra money from this, and without thinking touches the meteorite which quickly covers his fingers with moss, and before long spreads to cover all of him. It is an amusing role, but the saying "Don't quit your day job" has seldom been more apt. Stephen King is no actor, but it is fun to see him try and usually succeed in brief roles. Those of us who like King appreciate his efforts more than their result.

A further unusually large role is played by King in the 1994 mini-series of *The Stand*, where he pays Teddy Weizak, a character who appears is in several scenes and who actually does have some importance to the plot. But King's most noted performance in a movie is probably that in *It: Chapter 2* (2019), where he plays a pawn shop owner and sells Bill Denbrough's old bicycle. That his acting here was noted is probably largely because the film itself was much discussed and both praised and criticized. But far from everyone who watch it will recognize Stephen King. As an author, his name is far more well known than his image. But those of us who do know can sit smiling secretly in our cinema seats.

Personally, my favorite King movie appearance is that in *Maximum Overdrive* (1986). The film was scripted and directed by King, and most people including himself agree that it is quite awful. But if you take it for the apprentice work it is, I'd nevertheless call it worth seeing. In the film King plays a small role as a man trying to get cash from an ATM machine, but instead of handing him his money the machine insults him, calling him an asshole. King looks into the camera and yells to his wife, "Honey, this machine just called me an asshole!"

What King does is far from actual acting. His appearances in movies are what is called "cameo parts", and this in itself is far from new. The individual probably most famous for such appearances is probably Alfred Hitchcock (and perhaps in later years Stan Lee), whose cameo parts mainly consisted in his walking past the camera or stood reading a newspaper on a street corner. As far as I know Hitchcock never had any lines, nor did his acts ever influence the plot of the movies, as King's characters have done in several cases. The whole point of cameo appearances is primarily to amuse die-hard fans; they are in almost all cases not intended to contribute much to the movie as such.

In addition to their popping up in their movies, movie makers often like to put in so called "easter eggs", something King himself is fond of doing in his stories: unexpectedly there will turn up references to King himself or to his stories. For instance, in the film *Thinner* (1996), King plays a pharmacist named Mr. Banghor, which of course is a reference to King's hometown of Bangor. Those who know that this is where King lives will immediately react. Or take his guest appearance in the TV show *Sons of Anarchy*, one of the very few cameo roles King has had in a film not based on any of his own stories. After having praised the show, King was asked if he wouldn't like to be in it. He did, and plays a character who cleans up after someone has been killed. This time, his character is named Mr. Bachman. Those who know their King will recognize the name as that of his pen name Richard Bachman.

In spite of many of the films based on King's work being disappointing, it's still always fun to see him appear in them. Regardless of whether he does so just as a nameless person having a cup of coffee in the background, or as a named character with lines of dialogue. Remember his penchant for appearing in filmed versions of his work the next time you watch one of them. If you think someone on screen looks like Stephen King, chances are fairly good that it really is him.

Here is a list of the cameo roles in which King has appeared:

* *Knightriders* (1981): Man in the audience.
* *Creepshow* (1982): Jordy Verrill.
* *Maximum Overdrive* (1986): Man getting cash from an ATM machine.

- *Creepshow 2* (1987): Truck driver.
- *Pet Sematary* (1989): Priest.
- *Golden Years* (1991): Bus driver.
- *Sleepwalkers* (1992): Cemetery caretaker.
- *The Stand* (1994): Teddy Weizak.
- *Langoliers* (1995): Tom Holby (Craig Toomey's boss).
- *Thinner* (1996): Mr. Banghor (pharmacist).
- *The Shining* (1997): Conductor.
- *Storm of the Century* (1999): Lawyer in a TV commercial.
- *Rose Red* (2002): Pizza delivery man.
- *Kingdom Hospital* (2004): Johnny B. Good (janitor).
- *Kingdom Hospital* (2004): Same TV commercial as in Storm of the Century.
- *Fever Pitch* (2005): Himself.
- *Home Delivery* (2006): (animated): President of the US.
- *Sons of Anarchy* (2010): Mr. Bachman (cleaner).
- *Stuck in Love* (2012): Himself.
- *Under the Dome* (2013): Guest in a coffee shop.
- *Mr. Mercedes* (2017): Dead cook.
- *IT: Part 2* (2019): Pawn store owner.
- And here is a list of the voice cameos King has done:
- *Baseball* (1994): Documentary voice-over.
- *The Simpsons* (2000): Himself.
- *Frasier (2000)*: Brian (man who phones Frasier).
- *Kingdom Hospital (2004)*: AA sponsor (heard via phone)
- *Diary of the Dead* (2007): Radio preacher.
- La casa de papel/*Money Heist* (2021): Janitor (in the English-dubbed version).

The Film Director

At the start of the trailer for *Maximum Overdrive*, we hear a voice saying, "Hi, my name is Stephen King. I've written several motion pictures, but I want to tell you about a movie called *Maximum Overdrive*, which is the first one I've directed." As he speaks, we see Stephen King coming closer. He is bearded and behind him is a huge Green Goblin head, which makes this a good example on King himself referencing his reputation as a horror writer. He goes on to say, "A lot of people have directed Stephen King novels and stories, and I finally decided, if you want something done right, you ought to do it yourself." Finally he looks straight into the camera and says, "I'm gonna scare the hell out of you - and that's a promise!"

King both wrote the script for *Maximum Overdrive* (which is based on his short store "Trucks", included in *Night Shift*, Doubleday 1978) and directed the film, but despite this the movie scared nobody. Would King have done a better job if he hadn't been, as he himself says, "coked out of my mind"? Who knows? It is the only film King has directed, so there is nothing to compare it to, but it could hardly have been worse. And of course the fact is that King wasn't given the job because he is a great film maker or director. As he himself has stated in interviews, he got the job simply for being Stephen King. The film does offer a handful of scary scenes, and in some countries (one of them was Sweden) it was censored, but is it a good horror movie? Hardly.

The film stars Emilio Estevez, who plays a short-order cook at a Dixie Boy truck stop. Suddenly machines spring to life and take control of the world. We never learn what causes this, but are given a hint that it may be due to comet Rhea-M and its tail is passing close to the Earth; on the other hand, at the very end of the movie, King discloses that a UFO also has been shot down, so perhaps that caused it all. If not, what hade the UFO to do with anything, and why weren't we told more about it? As you may surmise, there are some unresolved questions about the film scrip as well.

Regardless of why, as I noted machines take control. They force humans to feed them gas and threaten to kill them if they don't. The fact that if you are hunted by a huge truck, you can turn sharply to get out of its way never seems to strike anyone, but that is just one of many illogical details we must ignore. We must also ignore that the role of newlywed Connie is played by Yeardley Smith, better known for being the voice of Lisa Simpson in *The Simpsons*, but it does make us feel as if we were in a satirical cartoon every time she has a line to say.

Filming was beset be numerous problems leading to delays. Radio operated cars kept breaking down and some scenes took much longer than planned. But the greatest and worst problem occurred on July 31, 1985, during filming in a suburb of Wilmington, North Carolina, when a radio-operated lawn mower ran amok and drove into a log which was used as a camera support. When it ran over the log, wooden splinters flew and photographer Armando Nannuzzi was hit so badly that he lost his right eye. Nannuzzi sued Stephen King for $18 million in damaged, but the suit was in the end settled out of court.

Maximum Overdrive was a colossal fiasco, both economically and critically. Even King himself has come to realize that the movie isn't very good, and nowadays even uses it as a warning example. Its star Emilio Estevez said in an interview that King had apologized repeatedly, and when asked in a *Vanity Fair* interview whether he ever regrets having accepted any role, Estevez mentions that in *Maximum Overdrive*: "Oh, God, yeah. I'm not speaking out of class because he knows it's a terrible movie, but Stephen King often talks about his one directorial experience on *Maximum Overdrive*, which I was in. The few times that I've connected with him over the years, he's like, "Can you forgive me for that?"

”I think at one point my mom said, “Why’d you do that movie?”
I said, “I wanted to work with Stephen King.” And she said,
“Couldn’t you have helped him paint his house?”

The film to a large extent was Stephen King. Fans liked to see
him in its trailer and on a poster where King holds all the actors like
puppets on strings. The poster read, ”Stephen King’s masterpiece
of terror directed by the master himself.” So when the movie
bombed, it was largely blamed on King. But it still has its fans, and
I am one of them: we like it simply because it is so bad it becomes
irresistibly entertaining. Incidentally, another fan of the movie is
King’s son Joe Hill, who has even suggested a remake where a
computer virus turning automatic cars into killing machines.
Opinions as to whether this was a serious suggestion or just a
sarcasm vary, but in either case I suspect the project might be a
difficult sell. On the other hand, stranger things have happened in
Hollywood.

It should come as no surprise that King also in this case connected
the film to other writings of his. One of them actually gave me
gooseflesh. When the film was made, King reasonably had no idea
of what future importance it would have, but early on a text is shown
onscreen to give some explanation for what happens:

”On June 19th, 1987, at 9:47 A.M. EST, the Earth passed into
the extraordinarily diffuse tail of Rhea-M, a rogue comet. According
to astronomical calculations, the planet would remain in the tail on
the comet for the next eight days, five hours, twenty-nine minutes,
and twenty-three seconds.”

Two details in this associate to other things in King’s life and
writings. The first of them is the name of the comet, Rhea-M. Both
in *The Eyes of the Dragon* and in the fourth Dark Tower novel,
Wizard and Glass (Donald M. Grant, 1997), we meet the witch Rhea
of Cöos. The second thing, and the one that gave me a startle, is the
date at the beginning of the text: June 19, 1987. Twelve years later,
to the day, on June 19, 1999, Stephen King was hit by a car and very
close to dying. A thing like that can make you wonder. Was it just by

chance that King chose that particular date, or did he have some kind of premonition? You choose.

After *Maximum Overdrive*, King has never again directed a movie, and he often brings it up as an example of how not to do so. Will he ever make a second attempt? Only King himself knows, but when someone asks him why he hasn't directed a second one, he usually answers: "Just watch *Maximum Overdrive*."

The Rock Star

We play music as well as Metallica writes novels.

–Dave Barry

The Rock Bottom Remainders, or, as the group was first called, just The Remainders, was formed by Kathi Kamen Goldmark in the fall of 1991. This was when she first asked a group of writers if they would be interested in forming a rock band with her. The band would consist of well known authors and would perform in order to contribute to some book-related charity, but at that time she had not decided on which. She sent her invitation via fax, which was the fastest form of written communication before e-mail and similar electronic means existed.

Stephen King was invited to join the band on January 11, 1992. By then the band had decided on calling themselves The Remainders, after having rejected other book industry related names like The Blurbs, Hard Cover, Cheap Trade Edition, Seamless Prose, and Finally in Paperback. The adopted name was first proposed by Michael Dorris, and is derived from "remaindered books", which is the trade term for unsold volumes which are put on sale at reduced prices. But two weeks later, someone discovered that there already was a band with that named, and so they became The Rock Bottom Remainders.

The band gave its first performance on May 25, 1992, playing acoustic rock at the American Booksellers Association Freedom of Speech gala at Anaheim Convention Center. They followed that gig with two further performances the same day at Cowboy Bookie, where one of them was filmed and later released on VHS tape. During the VHS movie release party in September, the group met again and began discussing further performances.

Stephen King had put the question to the others already in June: would The Rock Bottom Remainders play again? King took it further and suggested a tour with performances in cities like New York, Washington, D.C., Atlanta, Miami, and New Orleans. In his suggestion, King wrote, "The possibilities are endless. Someone might get an idea for a book, someone might get a bad case of the dribbling shits from a bad cheeseburger gobbled at a roadside Shoney's outside of Tired Rectum, Alabama." He had no idea of how right he was. But backstage during a gig at 328 Performance Hall in Nashville, Tennessee, on May 28, 1993, just an hour before they were due on stage, Stephen King himself did come down with the "dribbling shits". I the book *Mid-Life Confidential: The Rock Bottom Remainders Tour America with Three Chords and an Attitude* (by Kathi Goldmark, Robert Fulghum, Al Kooper, Barbara Kingsolver, Dave Barry, Ridley Pearson, Roy Blount, Amy Tan and Stephen King, Viking, 1994), he tells about sitting in one of two incredibly ugly toilet stalls without doors (to prevent visitors from taking drugs), talking to an usher who wonders if he is really the author of *The Shining* and *The Dead Zone*.

So King got his way and during 1993 The Rock Bottom Remainders toured the US. They called their tour "Three Chords and an Attitude" and performed in eight cities during the ten day trip in May. Their playlist consisted of 30 songs, out of which King sang on six: "Teen Angle", "Susie-Q", "Stand by Me", "Who Do You Love", "Last Kiss" and "Endless Sleep".

During the years since, band members have come and gone; even during the tour itself some members were switched. The group continued performing, but never regularly. In 1998 they issued a double CD entitled *Stranger Than Fiction* on Kathi Kamen Goldmark's label Don't Quit Your Day Job Records. The songs were called "Chapters" and the band members "The Wrockers", a combination of Writers and Rockers. It is perhaps not surprising that their record did not become a best seller.

In 2012, Amy Kamen Goldmark died of breast cancer, and after their memorial concert for her a month later The Rock Bottom Remainders was dissolved. But they again performed at the Tucson

Festival of Books in March, 2015, and occasional further performances have featured the band, irregularly and in changing constellations. Those who have had the time and inclination have joined, others not. Their last performance at the time of writing was on June 18, 2022, at the Nantucket Book Festival, but that time Stephen King did not join the band.

Apart from the VHS tape and the double CD published by the band I want to recommend two books to those wanting to learn more of the group. Both have unusually long titles. The first one, already mentioned, covers the band tour in 1993: *Mid-life Confidential: The Rock Bottom Remainders Tour America with Three Cords and an Attitude.* The later book is called *Hard Listening: The Greatest Rock Band ever (of Authors) Tells all* and is written by Sam Barry, Stephen King, Amy Tan, Dave Barry, Greg Iles, James McBride, Matt Groening, Mitch Albom, Ridley Pearson, and Scott Turow (Sam Barry Publishing, 2018). It is available as an interactive eBook and contains essays, thoughts, conversations, photos and both sound- and video recordings, all giving readers a glimpse into the lives of the authors.

One not unimportant question remains. Can Stephen King really sing? Well, though it does pain me to do so, I have to state that I don't think he ought to stop writing in order to pursue a success in music. I had the opportunity to sec him on stage during a publisher's party in London in 2006, when he visited Britain to promote *Lisey's Story*, when he rather reluctantly accepted an invitation to go on stage to sing with the house band. And sing he did, but not really at a level that would support a career change.

Still, I feel confident that The Rock Bottom Remainders will give more concerts. But I refrain from guessing when, where, or who will be in the band. We will know when it happens.

Interviewing a King 1

During the summer of 2001 I began exploring my chances of interviewing Stephen King for my website "Lilja's Library – The World of Stephen King", which I have kept up since 1996. The answer I received was that King currently gave no interviews. Optimist that I am, I chose to interpret this as me still having a chance – so I kept asking at regular intervals and every time was politely declined, with references to "He doesn't have the time right now", or "He has already given so many interviews about [insert title of book or film that was current when I asked] and declines doing any further". I respected the replies but refused to give up. Then finally, to be exact on June 15, 2006, I was given the reply I had been hoping for since five years. King agreed to an interview, and with me, Hans-Åke Lilja! This was magic!

The next step was finding a time that suited us both. Or, rather, one that suited King. I would have accepted any time and any day. If the time happened to clash with something else I had planned, I would happily have postponed it, whatever it might have been. I was certainly not going to say, "Sorry, no, I'm busy right then", when I had finally gotten a yes. It took six months before a definitive time was set, but in early January I learned at I would be able to do the interview on January 10, 2007.

The day arrived and I was ready. I had sent the rest of the family out of our house. I had written a list of questions to ask. I had prepared taping our conversation. Then the phone rang …

I answered and heard Stephen King's voice. "Hello, Hans? Steve King …"

Saying I was nervous would be an understatement, and I realize how strange it must seem when I write that after a while all nervousness left me. Obviously I was probably still more nervous than when I talk to anyone else on the phone, but King is very easy to talk to. He makes you feel very much at ease, and in the end we spoke for three quarters of an hour and I managed to ask more or less all of the questions I had prepared before we hung up. The following pages is a transcription of our conversation.

The interview was made on January 10, 2007. King's most recent book was *Lisey's Story*, which was published October 24, 2006.

Some names and expressions used in the interview may need a brief explanation:

- Marsha DeFilippo was Stephen Kings assistant and the moderator of the discussion forum on his webpage.

- Frank Muller was a very highly regarded audiobook reader.

- "Tabby" is Tabitha King, Stephen King's wife.

- "Dollar babies" is the term for movie rights to stories King sells for one dollar to film students and other non-professionals.

- Peter (whose last name was Straub) was an author in collaboration with whom Stephen King wrote two novels: *The Talisman* and *Black House*.

Stephen King: Hello Hans? Steve King...

Lilja: So, how are you feeling? Have you recovered from your accident?

Stephen King: Well, I think that if it had happened to me when I was 40 instead of 50 I might be all better but I get sore and I have a fair amount of pain in the hip and the leg but it doesn't keep me down much. I walk about three and a half miles a day and they told me, "Use it or you're gonna lose it", but mostly I feel just terrific. I'm great.

Lilja: I'm glad to hear it.

Having a website I wonder, how do you feel about all the websites about you that's out there on the Internet?

Stephen King: Well, I don't go much. I go to yours because it's always interesting, there is always a lot to look at .

Lilja: Thank you!

Stephen King: And sometimes I peek at The Dark Tower sites to see what's going on there and every now and then I'll be like a ghost and sniff around my own website. You know, I tell you what, it's a fun thing to do to go to those places because, as Amy Tan says, when you go and you check on what people are saying about you it's like being at a party and overhearing people say things and the things they say are fairly nice.

Lilja: Do you ever feel like contacting the people that have the sites and correct them if something is wrong or unfair?

Stephen King: No, I mean every now and then it's like... I was looking at the thread on *Lisey's Story* on the Stephen King website and there were several people that said, "Well jeez if Scott was so sick why didn't he go to that pool and get better?" and I got in touch with Marsha and said, "Will you tell these people that he couldn't do that because the long boy was laying across the path?". You see stuff like that and you say, "Jeez does these people really read or not?" Anyway, she put it on there but you could spend your life going to websites and looking at what people are saying about you and it would kind of slow me down and it would make me very self-conscious, so a lot of times I don't do it.

Lilja: I did a Google search on your name and I got about 40 million hits...

Stephen King: Wow!

Lilja: So, there are a lot of sites out there.

Stephen King: See, that is scary to think of that. What can they all have to say?

Lilja: Well, you have done a lot.

Stephen King: I have. I have done a lot and I don't know if that is a good thing or a bad thing but it's the way I am.

Lilja: It's definitely a good thing!

Stephen King: Well, good. Thank you.

Lilja: Do you feel the pressure? I read somewhere that people expected you to respond to questions on your official site. Do you feel a pressure to interact with the fans?

Stephen King: I don't particularly. I would rather that they think of me as Santa Claus. That I'm paying attention to their little lists but I can't respond to everything in person. I'd like to think that they know that I know what's going on and to some extent I do but as I say, if I paid attention to everything I wouldn't have time to write books and that's what most people want.

Lilja: Yes, I think everyone wants that if they have to choose.

I understand that *Blaze* will be out soon.

Stephen King: Yeah. I hope so. I mean that was a funny thing because I have been thinking about that book off and on for a while and every time I would think about it...you know I did the early books as Richard Bachman books and this is going to be a Bachman because it came from the same time. It was written right before *Carrie* and finally I thought to myself...the reason I've never done it was because, in my memory at least, it was a tearjerker of a book, you know it was kind of sentimental and just kind of...every now and then I think of what Oscar Wilde said about *The Little Match Girl*. He said that it's impossible to read about the little match girl without weeping tears of laughter and...you know something that is so sad it's actually funny.

And I felt that way a little bit about this Philip Roth book *Every Man*, you know I'm thinking, "that's ridiculous, this is so sad it's really quite funny" but I've got a kind of a black sense of humor too.

Lilja: Why did you decide to release it as a Bachman book?

Stephen King: I read it again. And I thought... well, the first thing that I thought was I've got to look at this if I can still find it, if anybody can find it because I've got this thing now, This Haven Foundation which is supposed to help freelance artists. You know about the Frank Muller situation?

Lilja: Yeah...

Stephen King: He had this horrible motorcycle accident and it turned out he had no money. He had no insurance. He had no backing. He owed the IRS, the Internal Revenue Service. He owed them money for back taxes. He was just a mess and he had this one kid and another kid on the way that he just found out about like three or four days before this accident. And he was never gonna be... I mean he's totally fucked up. Pardon my French but he's totally screwed up.

He's never gonna work again and there was no money. So, we set up the Wavedancer Foundation for him and we could never really get any traction because the amount of money was so high and I just kept thinking, it drove me crazy, I'm thinking if this has happened to Frank, think of all the other freelancers who are out there who probably don't have much, they are almost living hand to mouth, day to day. So we started this thing The Haven Foundation at the time of the reading I did with Jo Rowling and John Irving at Radio City Music Hall.

And the idea was to help writers and artists who were down on their luck and we gotta have some money to start with, we gotta have start up money so, I'm thinking to myself. I need a book, I need to publish a book and copyright it to The Haven Foundation and all the money can go to this thing because I don't need any more money, you know. I guess everybody could use it but right now I don't exactly need it anymore.

So, *Blaze* was what occurred to me and I thought, "Well, it's probably not good enough, why not look at it again and see?". So I did and I was wrong about it, it's really a good book. So, I rewrote it and I did it kind of, it was very funny to get the manuscript because it was done in my wife's old typewriter. Tabby claims that I married her for a typewriter. She had a nice little Olivetti, portable typewriter, very sturdy and I wrote *Carrie* on it, *Blaze* and a bunch of other stuff as well. I guess I wrote "Shawshank" on that typewriter too, on a kitchen table in Boulder.... I went ahead and I rewrote it and sent it in. And they like it at Scribner's so we're going to do it.

Lilja: And you're going to sell it through Haven Foundation?

Stephen King: Yeah, the money will go to Haven. And that way we'll have a certain amount in that fund to start with and we'll do some fundraisers. I did a political thing with John Grisham for a senatorial candidate in September because anybody who is against George Bush's Iraq policy is my friend.

Lilja: Yeah, I heard you talk about that...you got your wish.

Stephen King: Yeah, he got elected. He is a good guy. Bush met him and said, "How is your boy?" because Jim Webb's boy is fighting in Iraq and Webb said, "That's between my boy and me". Kind of spanked his nose. Not his business.

Lilja: You also wrote a story called "The Fifth Quarter" under the name John Swithen.

Stephen King: I did.

Lilja: Have you used other names?

Stephen King: No.

Lilja: Would you tell me if you had?

Stephen King: Actually at this point I would but I never have. The Swithen thing... at that time I was publishing stories all the time in *Cavalier* and this story wasn't like the horror stories. It's this hardboiled crime thing and I had a story in the previous issue and it was really like the pulp writers who used to use all different names in the 50's cause they poured that stuff out and that was my time to just pour stuff out so I used the John Swithen name but I never used it again. I didn't really like it. Have you seen the thing that they did of "The Fifth Quarter" for the *Nightmares & Dreamscapes*?

Lilja: Yes, I have seen it.

Stephen King: Not bad.

Lilja: The series was very good. I'm sad to hear that it probably won't be a second season.

Stephen King: I don't know, I don't think so. I don't really know. I mean it did pretty well for them. They're going to do *The Talisman.*

Lilja: What are your feelings about them turning *The Talisman* into a TV series?

Stephen King: I'm glad somebody's doing it. I mean it seems to me that that's the way to do it, as a miniseries because nobody could ever make it work as a movie, there was too much stuff in there and you know Spielberg had it for the longest time and those were the only tough movie negotiations that I ever had. Because Spielberg at that time had a boss named Sid Sheinberg at Universal Pictures and Sid Sheinberg kind of inserted himself into things and he was very rude and very, very hardnosed because I don't think he really wanted Spielberg to do that. At that time Spielberg was still young, he was really enthusiastic about all these things and he would buy a lot or things and let them sit. And Sheinberg was afraid that was what would happen to *The Talisman* and of course it was because it has been there for like twenty years.

Lilja: Yeah, I read that they even bought it before the book was released.

Stephen King: Yeah, I think they did... I think they did.

Lilja: I understand that a lot of fans are worried that it won't be possible to translate it into a successful movie because it has such a rich story.

Stephen King: I don't think it'll be the same. I have seen some of the scripts and the scripts concentrate pretty much on Jack Sawyer's relationship with Wolf and there's a lot more to the book than that but I think that they're kind of concentrating on that relationship. I think it will probably look nice and that it will have a story to it. Will it satisfy the fans? And between you and me and between everybody who reads your website, I have my doubts. We'll see.

Lilja: Are you concerned about how the movies turn out?

Stephen King: No...[laughs]

Lilja: No? You let them go when you...

Stephen King: No, I'm not concerned about that at all. [laughs]

The books are still always there. It's like what James M. Cain said, the book doesn't change and the movies... you know... *1408* is done and the trailer is terrific and... it looks like *The Shining* only hot instead of cold so maybe it'll be a great movie and everybody will make money and everybody will be happy. John Cusack's in it and I love him as an actor, I respect him very much. Samuel L. Jackson is the hotel manager. He looks terrific and the hotel looks terrific so all those things but... so maybe it's a success and that's terrific. But suppose it's junk. Then it's gone in two weeks. And that's the end of it. But I'm always just interested. I approach it as a fan and I know that there are writers who, what can I say, they kind of hover over things, the book is their little baby and in some cases I can understand that. It's like Charles Frazier who wrote... you know... the book and then it became a movie with Nicole Kidman and *Cold Mountain*.

The guy has only written two books in his career, of course he was concerned, you know. Ross Lockridge only wrote one book and then he killed himself. I don't know if he killed himself because the movie was so bad... it might have been. Elizabeth Taylor was in it and Montgomery Cliff... but you only have that one baby. You get really, really concerned. Did you read Scott Smith's book *A Simple Plan*?

Lilja: No, I haven't read that one.

Stephen King: Did you see the movie that Sam Raimi did out of it?

Lilja: No.

Stephen King: Ah, it's great. It's a great movie and it's a great book but the thing is Scott Smith who wrote the book spent six years dicking around with the screenplay because it was his only book. Now he's got another book out. It's a horror novel called *The Ruins* and that's a really nice book too. I mean it's not nice, it's scarier than hell, but, you know.. for me I write a lot of books and I'm always interested in what the movies are gonna be. It's like the Dollar Babies. I do it because I want to see what comes out. I'm like a kid with a chemistry set.

Lilja: Yeah, it's been a lot of Dollar Babies done lately.

Stephen King: Yeah and they're fun. Some of them are ridiculous and some of them are really terrific.

Lilja: Yeah, I saw a Russian version of "Battleground", I don't know if you have seen it?

Stephen King: No, I haven'.

Lilja: It's animated, very funny.

Stephen King: I'll have to get Marsha to send me one but you know there's also a Claymation version of "The Sun Dog" and it's a riot.

Lilja: I've heard about that one but never seen it.

Stephen King: They've done an off Broadway play of *Carrie* and Carrie is played by a transvestite and it's... I haven't seen it yet and it's closed but I think it will reopen. It was quite successful. Somebody said to me, "Do you care that they kind of like turned this thing into a, almost like a camp comedy?" and I said, "No". I really don't care about that it has that element in it and so what. Let's see what comes.

Lilja: If you try enough times something good will come from some of them.

Stephen King: Exactly, I mean a guy like Frank Darabont comes along and you know, Frank and I have stayed tight over the years. He's going to start with *The Mist* in, I think, about six weeks. And that's exciting.

Lilja: Are you more excited about some films then others?

Stephen King: Sure. I'm excited about *The Mist*, I was always kind of pumped to see what happened with *Cujo* and of course *Misery*. I was very excited about *Misery* because it was William Goldman that was doing the script and you know, he's been an idol of mine most of my life. *Dolores Claiborne* with Kathy Bates again and Jennifer Jason Leigh. I was very interested to see what would happen.

Some of them were disappointments you know... *Needful Things* for instance but some of them are really fun to watch and I'm easy to please.

Lilja: In some movies you have small cameos. Is that something you enjoy doing?

Stephen King: Yeah, it's OK if I've got the time to do it. I mean I'm not a really great actor. I could probably, you know, if I had the right agent and everything I could have a career as a minor character actor sort of Whit Bissell in the old 50's movies but... I have never been really great at it but it's kind of fun to do that. Frank wanted me to actually play a fairly major part in *The Mist*. But I said, "you know, I can't do that. You're planning to go and shoot this in some God awful place like New Zealand and I just can't uproot my like life that".

Lilja: It's always nice to see you pop up in the movies though.

Stephen King: Thank you.

Lilja: I understand that you have another book ready called *Duma Key*?

Stephen King: Duma Key is done in first draft and it's kind of a glorious mess right now and needs to be shorter but it's a good story.

It's the first of the stories I have written that are set in Florida. We have been coming down here for about eight years and I feel comfortable writing about it. Finally I said to myself, "You write all these books about Maine because it's comfortable for you and it's easy but sometimes good things come from discomfort". So I tried to do the best that I could, it's a scary story that's kind of sweet.

Lilja: Can you reveal anything about the plot?

Stephen King: Sure, it's about a construction worker who is involved in a terrible accident. He lives in the northern part of the United States, Minnesota, and he's hurt very badly and loses an arm, sustains head injuries and is not expected to live but he does and he comes out of a coma and because of the head injuries he has uncontrollable rages and memory lapses. It's very difficult and his wife divorces him so he decides he's going to move to Florida but he's also thinking about suicide just because of his pain and because he doesn't like being angry all the time and this psychiatrist kind of talks him out of it and one of the things he says is, "Is there anything that you do that you can use as a kind of buffer against this depression? Is there any kind of new life for you besides working on buildings?" and this guy says, "I used to draw, I used to paint a little bit" and the guy says, "Well, try that" and he discovers that, after this injury, that he is really a very talented painter and he moves to Florida and he starts to paint these pictures and then strange things start to happen with the pictures. They have this power so that sometimes if he paints things into the world they kind of appear and if he paints things out they disappear, including people. And there is something going on, on this island, this Duma Key that is actually amping that talent up and making it stronger because there is something wrong there. That's the real basis of the story.

Lilja: Do you expect it to be out this year?

Stephen King: No, I don't think so. I've got to work on it and I kind of like... you know what happens to me is, I say to myself, "I've got to rewrite this book and there's a lot of work involved because it's too long" and I think to myself, "I don't wanna do that, I'd rather write something new". So that's what I'm doing, I'm working on something new.

Lilja: Can you reveal anything about that?

Stephen King: Well, it's a story called "The Gingerbread Girl" and it's going to be long, I think...I don't think it's gonna be a novel but I think it's gonna be pretty long, probably not as long as "Shawshank" or "The Body" or those things but probably pretty long.

It's one of those stories that falls into a no-man's land. It's too long to be a short story and get published in a magazine but it's too short to be a novel.

Lilja: Speaking of that are you planning a new collection soon where it might fit?

Stephen King: Somebody was asking me about that and I don't know what I've got that hasn't been published, I'd have to think about it. If I went to Marsha and said, "Find out how many short stories are uncollected" she could do that but I don't know how many that is.

There's a story in Tinhouse called "Memory" but that's really the first chapter of *Duma Key* all kind of dressed up.

Lilja: Yeah, I remember reading that, that it was an excerpt from *Duma Key*. That was a very good story.

Stephen King: It's pretty good. It's about the guy's accident. And there's a story called "Lisey and the Madman" but that's from *Lisey's Story* so those two are out. I don't wanna do those but there are a few other ones. There's a story in Playboy last month called "Willa".

Lilja: Is "Willa" something you'd want to expand?

Stephen King: No, I don't think so but I was still sort of under the influence of *Lisey's Story*. I had a wonderful time writing *Lisey's Story*, it was kind of magic for me and there seemed to be a little of that magic left over at the end and it went into "Willa".

Lilja: "Lisey's Story" is a very nice book. One of your best books if I may say so.

Stephen King: I think it's THE best book.

Lilja: Yeah?

Stephen King: Yes, I do. Yeah, I think it's the best one and... you just never know. You sit down to work on a book and then when I was done with it I said to myself, "I don't really wanna write another book because it won't be as good". I mean it's like if you read a really good book, you put it on the shelf and you feel sad because you say to yourself, "I'm gonna read another book but I know it won't be as good as this one".

Lilja: Do you feel that when you're done or do you feel it in the process, that this is about to be something very good?

Stephen King: You just feel it. You know when it's going along day by day that it's really, really good and you don't know why... you just kind of like...write it and say, "boy I hope this will stick that way". But...I never had a book quite like *Lisey* and it was funny how that worked out because when I wrote most of it I was really sick a lot of the time. I had pneumonia and I picked up one of these hospital infections so that when I got out of the hospital I was just nauseated all the time, I couldn't keep food down, I felt like crap. The book was just angelic... So that was good but I actually literary wrote *Lisey* in between running to the bathroom to vomit what I had eaten last and finally I shook whatever it was I had. And the book just never really lost that magic for me and usually you write a book and you usually feel pretty good about it when you're writing it. I usually feel like "Goddamn, this is good, this is great" and then it comes to a point when you have to work on it again and you say, "oh, what a pile of shit this was, what were you thinking?". You know you always feel a little bit like you fell short but I never felt that way with *Lisey*. I felt good about that book.

Lilja: Do you work more now than you did before?

Stephen King: It comes and it goes. It comes and goes in streaks. I had a time last year in January and February when we were down here in Florida and I couldn't really seem to get anything going. It just... nothing really seemed to work. It all fell apart like in my hands like tissue paper and this year it's like I can't do anything wrong, I really feel like I'm in a groove. I should not say that, now it will change.

Lilja: I hope it won't.

Stephen King: I hope it won't either.

Lilja: Do you work on several projects at the same time, or...?

Stephen King: Not anymore. I'm too old for that and you know it used to be that I would work on something fresh in the morning and then I would rewrite at night but I also used to get loaded at night. I used to drink a lot and that's kinda like... it's a medicine for...I don't know...insecurity or something because I'd work and be a little bit loaded and I say, "Damn this is good" and it wasn't always, so...

Lilja: It's better when you're not drunk then?

Stephen King: Yeah!

Lilja: Yeah, I'm glad to hear that.

Stephen King: Now instead of working morning and night I have a tendency to work mostly in the morning... once every two or three weeks I'll push everything aside and I write one of these Entertainment Weekly columns and... I don't know... that's a little bit harder than it used to be. You just want them to be good and at the same time you want them to feel casual and kinda off the cuff, it's not easy to achieve that all the time but the column's been kind of fun. It's certainly given me a chance to do something different and that's OK.

Lilja: Is it hard to work under a deadline?

Stephen King: It's strange. I don't know if you actually say it's hard but sometimes it's kinda fun. They asked me one time if I would do a column on a movie about the Red Sox. I'm trying to think...Drew Barrymore was in that and...

Lilja: I think you were in it as well?

Stephen King: Yeah, I was in it. Yeah, that's right. I did have a little cameo in that. It was called *Fever Pitch.*

I'm in the movie and I can't remember what it was. But that is because I didn't have any lines. I didn't really get a close up.

Lilja: Was that pitch just for the movie or did you do it for... was it real?

Stephen King: They just did the movie and they asked me if I would do this thing where they could film me throwing out the first pitch at this game and that was already scheduled with the Red Sox so I said, "Sure, why not. Knock yourselves out".

So that was kinda fun but then the people from Entertainment Weekly called me and said, "Will you write a piece about this? They'll screen the movie for you today but we would need the piece tonight because we're going to press and we wanna do it in this issue". So I saw the movie and I wrote the piece that night in about an hour and a half which was all the time I had. And that was kinda fun. That was like being back in collage again and having a deadline for a paper or something and sometimes when somebody puts you under that kind of stress you do good work. So you respond to the challenge. I mean I like to think of myself not as this big rich best-selling writer but just as a craftsman, somebody who does this day by day.

Lilja: I hear also that there will be a third book about Jack Sawyer?

Stephen King: I hope so. I've gotta try to clear some space for that but that was always the plan.

Lilja: You always planned to do three books?

Stephen King: Well, I don't think we always planned to do three books, we planned to do one. And then at some point I think that I suggested to Peter that we do another book, a follow-up. You know in some ways it was a great book, I really enjoyed that book, I enjoyed the process. I enjoyed the process the second time even more than the first because it seemed to me to actually be a richer book in some ways and just... the funny thing about... it's the same for writers as it is for readers when you go back and revisit characters that you've written about before, they become real in your imagination and it's like meeting old friends.

So, we really sort of enjoyed that book but it was an unlucky book because it was scheduled to be published on September 13, 2001 and two days before that they hit the World Trade Center and you know Peter and I had been scheduled to do this big publicity swing, we were going to do the talk shows, do signings and this and that and the other thing and everything just got cancelled. The book... it was almost like a book that didn't happen. Because of all the tragedy that went around and you know I called Peter on the phone and I said, "I don't think anybody's gonna wanna read about a supernatural cannibal after what just happened". And the book sold pretty well but it didn't sell at the time, nothing did really.

Lilja: Was it harder to write the second book then the first book?

Stephen King: No.

Lilja: Easier?

Stephen King: No, it was about the same. It was just a real pleasure. And working with somebody else lightens the load. If it's someone that you see eye to eye with. I mean Peter is a great guy and I've always really gotten along with him, it's like he's my big brother in a way so it was kinda like, I think, my idea that we do the follow-up with *Black House* and with the third one, the way *Black House* turned out, we never had any question that there is to be another book. It's just a question of trying to find the time.

Lilja: Have you planned out the plot of the third book?

Stephen King: Ah...[laughs] ...it's there, I mean sometimes you just know. It's there just waiting for us, you know. Because Jack is hurt, goes over to the Territories and the way things are left is that he'll be OK if he's over there on the other side but if he comes back to our world he will sicken and die in short order so of course you have to put him in some sort of situation where he has to come back and then the clock is ticking.

Lilja: You are also collaborating with John Mellencamp on a musical.

Stephen King: Right.

Lilja: Is that very different than writing a book?

Stephen King: We've got a guy and I'm not going to mention his name but we got a guy who looks like he's going to direct it. I'm not telling you who it is because he hasn't signed up for it yet but he's going to come down here. He's talked to John and he's going to talk to me. We're going to have lunch and talk about some things at the end of this month and then I would like to go back to work on that again, well I take that back. I worked on it so much, it's been through so many drafts that I don't really wanna go back to work on it again but maybe if I can do what this man feels comfortable with then we can get the thing off up on stage out of town. Maybe in some place like Houston or southern California and if people actually come to it and like it then we can bring it to Broadway which was always the goal.

Lilja: Do you think it might be released in some kind of book form or on DVD or something for people not living in the US?

Stephen King: I don't know, I don't think so. But my idea... what I always said to John when we were just sort of slogging along and there was like nobody got it and I said, "You know if worse things comes to worst, John, what we do is we release a package that contains the CD with all the music and the script for the play and people will buy that".

Lilja: That would be nice.

Stephen King: Yeah, it would and something like that may come along eventually and there'll be CDs with the music. The music is terrific.

Lilja: Yeah, John is a really good musician.

Stephen King: Yeah, it's very sweet and at the same time some of the pieces rock really hard and it's something that's really not been done on Broadway in my experience. You know there are plays that are kind of like the Andrew Lloyd Webber deal where everybody sings all the parts and there are musicals that here in the states we call Juke Box musicals and the closest thing to what we've got is Jersey Boys which used to be autobiography, it's the biography of the Four Seasons which is a story with a lot of music in it but that's like, almost like a bioplay you know and this is fiction and drama. It's interesting it's a kind of a one of a kind thing right now.

Lilja: You have tried to publish in a lot of formats like this musical, screenplays, eBooks, serial books and so on... Is there something left? Is there some media that you haven't tried?

Stephen King: Well, there's always the Internet. I was just delighted to read that Michael Connelly had done a kind of mini-movie of the first two chapters of his novel *Echo Park*. And he put it on YouTube and a lot of people watched it and it built interest in the book and I thought, "That's an interesting idea". So I can't really say, there are a lot of different possibilities. I have been approached with the idea of downloads for cell phones and I'm like, "Don't you guys realize that cell phones are the Devil?" [laughs]

Lilja: [laughs]

Stephen King: You kind of download it and get a copy on your phone... I don't know about that one but you know I'm open to any kind of a format and I'm always interested in things because it keeps you fresh. Some of the fans gets a little bit disgruntled but that's good, too, you know. I like to upset them. It's my job.

Lilja: I think it's great that you're trying a lot of different things. I wish you would continue with *The Plant* on your site though.

Stephen King: Oh, but the thing is, about *The Plant*, is I ran out of stories. It was a great idea and people downloaded it. I think that a lot of the press was kind of discouraging about the way that that worked financially because it made them nervous but actually it was a license to coin money. There were no production costs or anything. Well, you know, you run a website. And there's a certain amount of... you know, expense involved in keeping things like that up and running but it's nothing compared to this support system, the infrastructure that it takes to publish books.

Lilja: Speaking of publishing, it seems less and less of your books have been released in limited editions now. Is that something you have done deliberately?

Stephen King: They are releasing *Secretary of Dreams* now and Frank Darabont is really high on the idea of doing a limited edition of *The Mist*. I don't like them, I don't like them. I think they are books for rich people and they're elitist and the whole idea of limiteds... there's something wrong with it, you know. The idea that people want a book that they can kind of drool over or masturbate on, I don't know what it is they want with these things but it's like they get this book and it's this beautiful thing and they go like, "Don't touch it, don't... oh God it's worth a thousand dollars, he signed it" and all this and my idea of a book that I like is when someone comes up to me at an autographing and you got this old beat-to-shit copy of *The Stand* and they say, "I'm sorry it looks this way" and I go like, "I'm not". It means a lot of people have read it and enjoyed it.

Lilja: But often they look very good, the limiteds.

Stephen King: Well, they do but... on the other hand my mother used to say, "Handsome is as handsome does".

Lilja: That's true...

Stephen King: A thing is better looking when it's useful and... you know something you just put up on the shelf to just look at it. Isn't that weird?

I mean... the worst one in a way and I don't... this guy is gonna read this and be so bummed. This guy Jared Walters did *Salem's Lot* in a limited. He basically fucking wore me down because he would come back every six months or so and say, "Please, please, please, please" and I'm very vulnerable to that if people, I mean, if he'd come to me and said that he wanted to do a Dollar Baby I would say, "Yes" immediately but this guy wants to do this big huge book with this, I don't know, incredible binding done in some endangered species or something and finally the books come out and people like Frank Darabont and other collectors just loved that book and he wants to do *The Shining* next and so far I've just told him, "No". Because it'd be another book like *Salem's Lot*. It'll weigh twenty pounds, and people will put it on their shelf and look at it and they won't actually read it.

Lilja: But I have read that book and it was interesting to get a chance to read the parts that wasn't in the first edition.

Stephen King: Yeah, I know that but on the other hand if someone had suggested to me, "Why don't you put that up on the net, the stuff that wasn't in the first edition?" I would have done that. And then people could have gotten it for free.

It would be the same words. It just wouldn't be in that fancy thing. It's like... I don't know how to say this. It's like if you see some woman and you're really hot for her, you know. I mean you got to say to yourself is it the woman I'm hot for or is it just because she's wearing a certain expensive dress? I don't know...

Lilja: What do you think people will think when they hear the name Stephen King say 50 or 100 years from now?

Stephen King: I think that they'll have some vague memory of my work and some of the older ones will have read it and it's maybe that some of the books will last, it may be that *The Shining, Salem's Lot...* ahh... I'm hoping *Lisey's Story*. That some of these books may still be read but you know what? I think that you never know, you never know what's gonna happen. You have no clue. Nobody would have believed, people would have laughed in 1910 if somebody would have said Theodore Dreiser was going to be a writer that people remember and read. But I think that my faith might be sort of like Somerset Maugham's. He was a novelist who was read wildly in his time, everybody read Somerset Maugham and he's still the record holder in terms of films made from his books. 48 movies from different books and remakes and that sort of things. I'm close to that---

Lilja: Yeah, you must be very close to that---

Stephen King: I am, I'm close to that. But nowadays if you ask people who Somerset Maugham is they'll kinda go like, "Well, I guess he was a writer...", "The name is very familiar..." so I think that that might be my fate.

Lilja: Is that the fate you would like?

Stephen King: No, I think any writer would like to be remembered and somebody who's read, you know, somebody whose work stands the test of times, so to speak. But on the other hand as a person, I'll be dead and if there's no afterlife then I won't give a shit, I'm gone. And if there is an afterlife I got an idea that what goes on here is a very minor concern.

But you know, I'm built a certain way and the way I'm built is to try and give people pleasure. That's what I do. I want people to read the books and be knocked out and I'd like that to continue even after I stop.

Lilja: I'm sure it will.

Stephen King: No, I'm not sure.

Lilja: Definitely.

Well, it was very nice to talk to you.

Stephen King: Same here, very pleasant.

Interviewing a King 2

If I was surprised when I after five years of trying managed to secure an interview with King in 2007, I was considerably more surprised when I was granted a second interview only a little over a year later. Neither before nor after he talked to me had King ever agreed to be interviewed by any fan site, and now he would let me have a second talk with him. Unbelievable. I hope and believe that the reason for this was that he thought I had done well the first time, or at least not too badly, and that I had asked him interesting and relevant questions. Perhaps he appreciated not only having to talk about his latest book or film.

I remember him saying that he didn't think we would have very much more to talk about, given that we had spoken only about a year previously. I ensured him that we did, and in the end we talked for just about half an hour this time.

The interview was made in February, 2008. King's most recent book was *Duma Key* (Scribner, 2008) which was published January 22, 2008.

Some names and expressions used in the interview may need a brief explanation:

- Peter David and Robin Furth are the authors of the graphic version of *The Dark Tower* series. Robin also works as a research assistant for Stephen King, and is an expert *The Dark Tower* books.

- Jae Lee (with Richard Isanove) was the illustrator for first series of *The Dark Tower* in graphic version.

Lilja: Hi Steve! How are you? Fine?

Stephen King: Yes, I am. I'm very well indeed.

Lilja: I just finished your last book *Duma Key* and first I wanna say that I really liked it.

Stephen King: Well, good, I'm glad.

Lilja: Was that one different to write since it was set in Florida compared to your other books?

Stephen King: You know, it was a hard book to write because I had a little idea at first of these two little dead girls that I kept seeing on this road at dusk. And that image actually never made it into the book but that was where I started and the rest of it just all sort of came out… for the day to day writing it was never a plot, it was never an outline so by the time I had finished it I had… you know these little sticky notes that people put up on their desks and things?

Lilja: Yeah.

Stephen King: I had those all over my computer, I could barely see the screen, I had them all over my desk, I had them on the walls…so I would try not to forget anything and when I got done I just had to laugh and I thought "boy I wrote that book by the seat of my pants" [laughs]

Lilja: [laughs] So it was harder to write than your usual book?

Stephen King: Ah….yeah, I think it was. You know, I write two different kinds of books. I write books that have a lot of plot which are difficult and then there are the ones that are just situations like *Cell* where you say to yourself "What would happen if everyone went crazy at the same time?" and you just kinda play that out. Those are a lot easier …

Lilja: I noticed that Edgar, the main character, is in a lot of pain in the book. Did you draw from your own experience when you wrote that?

Stephen King: I did but I thought that nobody would mistake Edgar for me since his injuries are so much worse than mine were. He loses his arm. But I know enough about pain to wanna write a little bit about that, to wanna write about getting better. The only time I have ever actually written about my own was in *On Writing* so it was a chance to explore some of that and basically what I wanted to write about that, was on my mind was… About three years after the road accident I had pneumonia. This was around the time of the National Book Award and I had an intestinal bug that was a hospital germ that I picked up and when I was done with all that it was like my memory kinda took a hit, it was hard to remember things and that was really scary and I wanted to write about that.

Lilja: You did a really good job. You really feel for Edgar when you read the book.

Stephen King: Well, thanks. The other thing is I have a friend, his name is Frank Muller, who read books on tapes, he read a lot of my books on discs and tapes and he had a motorcycle accident and he really… he is never gonna be normal again. I don't think he's ever going to regain his thought processes but one of the things about Frank is that you have to be careful around him now because he goes into rages. Apparently this is pretty common in frontal brain injuries. To get angry and strike out against the one they love so I thought I wanted to write about that too.

Lilja: In the book Edgar becomes a painter and you have also used painters quite often in your later work. Have you developed an interest in painting yourself?

Stephen King: I can't even draw a cat [laughs] but I like pictures and I have had some stuff to do with artists particularly with *The Dark Tower* books and I'm interested in the way they work but it was also a chance to get away from the idea of everyone saying "All you ever write about is writers". I like to write about what I know; there is a comfort level there. There are more ways to write about art and the creative impulses than just writing about writers. To me even after 35 years--most of my life--of writing stories, the process itself is a total mystery. I have no idea how creativity happens or why it happens or what it does to the person who creates it except it makes you feel good while it's going on.

Lilja: So you haven't started painting your own paintings?

Stephen King: No, I haven't started painting my own paintings but you know Edgar's paintings are like my work and that's one thing that nobody said in the reviews or the discussions of the book. Edgar paints sunsets, which are clichés and he changes them from clichés to something else by adding one object that has no business to be there. And what I do is that I write about ordinary people and add something that's surreal or horrible or out of place in the story and that changes everything so in that sense Edgar really is like me.

Lilja: Speaking of paintings. I really like the cover for the book. I think it's actually one of the best covers for your books.

Stephen King: Do you?

Lilja: Yes. Do you have a lot to say when it comes to the covers of your books or is that left to the publisher?

Stephen King: No, I got quite a lot to say about it and we talked about that and I said that I thought it would be great if they could have the ocean with a big shell in the foreground and some tennis balls so they got all those things in it.

Lilja: Have you done a lot of promotion for *Duma Key*?

Stephen King: No.

Lilja: No? I thought there was less than usual.

Stephen King: I didn't go out a lot, I'm working on a new book and I wanted to do that and I'm assuming it's gonna be a long book, a really long book. Like *The Stand* or *IT* or something like that I think. A very long book. And I talked to the people at the publisher and said, "You have your choice. Either I can work on this book and maybe you can have it in a year or two or I can go out and promote and do all these things that you want me to do and you won't". So eventually they saw reason.

You know I did this thing at Radio City with J.K. Rowling and she is a great person, she is very vivacious and she is very lively and very much with it but when we had a run through for the thing I could see that one of her publishers from Scholastic was talking to her and Jo Rowling came back to me and said "Can I talk to you for a minute?" and I said "Sure".

And she was really steamed and I said "What's the matter?" and she said "They don't understand do they? They really don't understand. They think these things write themselves". Because she told them she was coming to New York, she was going to do this benefit reading and then she was going to work on the 7th Harry Potter book and they took the opportunity to ask her to do all these other things and that's the fact, this goes back to that whole business of creativity and what it is and what it isn't. They don't understand. They think somehow that this stuff just occurs by magic.

Lilja: But you have spoiled your publishers with a lot of books over the years so they think you can write really fast.

Stephen King: Well, I can but I have to be left alone to do it.

Lilja: Do you like doing promotion if you have the time?

Stephen King: Hate it!

Lilja: Hate it? So you won't be going back to the UK for a tour any time soon?

Stephen King: I don't have any real plans to go back but you know I hate the promotion and when I go to the UK they really work me hard, they really want you out there, pushing… but the other side of it is that I love those people at Hodder and it's very difficult for me to say no to them.

Lilja: So, they just have to ask you in the right way then?

Stephen King: Yeah, exactly.

Lilja: You also have a collection of short stories coming out.

Stephen King: I do.

Lilja: Will it be out this year?

Stephen King: I think it's gonna come out in…November. We went back and forth about the title. I wanted to call it *Unnatural Acts of Human Intercourse.*

Lilja: Yeah, I remember reading about that and also *Pocket Rockets*?

Stephen King: Yeah.

Lilja: Are there usually this many titles flying around?

Stephen King: You know, books with short stories are hard to title unless you name them after one of the stories and when I finally settled on the title I thought, "gee, *Unnatural*

Acts of Human Intercourse, that is a really good title" but they had a shit-fit. [laughs]

Lilja: [laughs] Yeah, I read that the publisher thought they would have a really hard time promoting it.

Stephen King: Yeah, "We can't sell this, we blah, blah, blah" and I said "Well, look in your dictionary man, intercourse doesn't even have anything to do with sex". It's what we're doing right now. We're having a conversation back and forth.

Lilja: Yeah, I liked that title. I was hoping for it but I guess *Just Past Sunset* is good as well…

Stephen King: Yeah, it's like *Nightshift* and *Four Past Midnight*. It has some of that vibe to it so if they like that, it's fine.

Lilja: Is it easier to name books that aren't collections?

Stephen King: Yes! Cause the titles always kinda suggest themselves after a while. The only time I ever had a problem was the vampire book I wanted to call *Second Coming* and someone said it sounds like a sex manual.

Lilja: [laughs]

Stephen King: So, we ended up calling that one something else.

Lilja: Will all the previously published but uncollected stories be in the collection?

Stephen King: Now, I'm not supposed to talk to you about that very much… I think there's like 13 stories in the collection, which is a good number of stories for a collection of scary stories.

Most of them are the ones that have been published in magazines but haven't been collected. There is one story that is brand new that is called "N." Just the letter N with a period after it and that's a long story and you know, you could guess… The long stories like "The Gingerbread Girl" are gonna be in there and there is one other long one that hasn't been published yet that's called "A Very Tight Place" so those will be kind of the cornerstones and the anchors to it and the other ones … the stories that aren't going to be in there are the ones that developed into novels, "Lisey and the Madman" and "Memory". They won't be in there.

Lilja: The first story arc of *The Gunslinger* comic is finished. Are you happy with how it turned out?

Stephen King: I loved it.

Lilja: Yeah?

Stephen King: Yeah, I really loved it. They are going to do *The Stand* I think if we can work out arrangements.

Lilja: Yeah, I remember there were talks about *The Stand* about a year ago, or two.

Stephen King: Doubleday has the rights to most of that so it's gonna go on for a while before we get that worked out but hopefully it'll happen.

Lilja: You should also do *Eyes of the Dragon*. It would fit well as a comic.

Stephen King: Well, I'd like to do something original in that field at some point. You know cause there are a lot of those graphic novels things that I really like. There is one called *Y: The Last Man* that's really nice. And I'd really like to try that sometime.

Lilja: Yeah, it would be really interesting to see an original Stephen King comic. What are your feelings about the next story arc; *The Long Road Home*?

Stephen King: I like the way…well, first of all let me say this. The first issue is terrific and the way that the arc is outlined is very good. I like that a lot. It really just takes off from the previous one so that's nice. And Peter David and Robin Furth have really started to click and work together really well so I think it's gonna be OK. You can never tell because, it's like the movie, once a lot of people start working together it's always a little unpredictable what's going to happen but we'll see.

Lilja: How much input have you had in it since it's not based on something you have previously written?

Stephen King: Well, with the first one I had a lot of input because it was basically *Wizard and Glass* but my feelings about stuff like this are the same whether it's movies or something like a graphic novel. The comic books are very similar to movies in a lot of ways. They become more and more cinematic as years go by, wouldn't you agree with that?

Lilja: Yeah, I really like the widescreen format of the comics, that the frames are covering the entire page.

Stephen King: Yeah, and I love Jae Lee as an artist. I think he rocks!

Lilja: Yeah, he is very talented.

Stephen King: Yeah, terrifically talented guy. Very quiet, very modest but my idea is that either you get right in there and write the damn thing or you stand away and let people do their best work and don't… "too many cooks spoil the broth" as the saying goes and there you are.

Lilja: Yeah, I can't wait to see what they have done with it. Do you know if all the story arcs are mapped out? Have you given them some guidelines to navigate by?

Stephen King: Yeah, I gave them some overall guidelines and I can tell you what it is basically. You know the story *Wizard and Glass*, Roland and his friends are basically kids. They have just gotten their first guns and they are sent away to this cattle area called Mejis and they have all these adventures and then they go back and Roland actually shoots his mother by mistake. Which is a spoiler I guess technically but anyone who doesn't know that hasn't read the stories anyway so… The next time in chronological order we see Roland of Gilead is when he is in the desert chasing the Man in Black and all these years have gone by. We don't even know how many years but it's a lot more than a normal man's lifespan and what I said when we sat down with Marvel was "this is the area you wanna focus on", the young manhood of Roland and his friends with the overall story of The Crimson King and this guy who is working to overthrow all of civilization and they just took to that like ducks to water and started to build these arcs around that and I just thought it was terrific and after that I just kind of walked away from the project and I look at it and I'm really sort of an outsider at this point and that's fine. I gave them my little railroad trains to play with and they're doing their thing.

Lilja: Robin is very involved in *The Dark Tower* now; she knows probably more than you do?

Stephen King: She does, it's no probably about it.

Lilja: Some time ago there were also talks about a movie version of *The Dark Tower* by J.J. Abrams?

Stephen King: Yeah, I think they are still interested in that but you know for me it was a way of actually… how can I say this… it was a way of stopping a lot of requests and a lot of speculations I was getting from people. I'd get calls from producers "Have you sold this? Have you thought about selling this?" Fans would write and try to cast the movie, got this one to play Roland and that one… and all that stuff so… J.J. Abrams and Damon Lindelof and Carlton Cuse who are the people that do *LOST* came up to Maine and we had a roundtable discussion that Entertainment Weekly put on and Maine was the logical place to do it because I live there and J.J's wife comes from Brewer which is right across the river from where I live so… we started to talk about *The Dark Tower* and they expressed an interest and based off what I had seen of *LOST* they were just the people to do it and whether or not it ever gets made is another question because it would have to be something that would bend over an arc of many movies and in the case of *The Lord of the Rings* and the C.S. Lewis *Narnia* series… those experiments in what I call long form movies, long form cinema, has been very successful but then people tried the Philip Pullman thing, his dark material and that was a flop so it's risking a lot of money on a format that's very iffy so we'll see if anything happens but in the meantime I don't have to answer as many questions as I used to.

Lilja: What is your gut feeling about it? Could it be transformed into a movie?

Stephen King: Yeah, sure.

Lilja: I guess it was about the same time that you had the meeting with the people from *LOST* that there was a rumor that you were going to write an episode for *LOST*.

Stephen King: [laughs] Just rumors. I mean they got that pretty well in hand. There is a guy called Brian K. Vaughan who's a comic guy that has done some work for them and his been terrific. I think they got that well in hand.

Lilja: So you don't feel the urge to try?

Stephen King: Well, I'd never say never. I would think about it if it ever came up but so far it hasn't.

Lilja: Is there any other TV series that you felt like writing an episode for like you did with *The X-Files*?

Stephen King: Well, with *The X-Files*… that was kind of a strange experience because I was re-written so heavily by Chris Carter that it was really very odd, a very odd experience. I don't know whether, was it William Gibson who did an episode of *The X-Files* as well… one of those cyberpunk writers did one and I just wondered… I always thought I'd like to get in touch with him to find out what his experience was with Carter because I got re-written pretty exhaustively. You know I like TV and I like long form but as far as actually writing an episode of a show… I can't think of anything that is on TV right now that would interest me that way.

Lilja: It must be hard to write about characters that already have their history and you have to adapt very much to what's already happened.

Stephen King: Well it can be fun…

Lilja: Yeah?

Stephen King: No question about that but I'm more interested in original stuff I'd say.

Lilja: Speaking of original stuff, you're also working with John Mellencamp on the musical *The Ghost Brothers of Darkland County*.

Stephen King: It looks like it's actually going to be an out of town… We're gonna get this play up and running probably in April 2009. We're going to do another workshop this summer in New York, put the finishing touches on it and somewhere, probably on the east coast maybe Miami or Atlanta somewhere down south it'll be on next April I think, quite sure of that.

Lilja: Do you plan to release it as a DVD or something for people not living in the US?

Stephen King: [laughs] Ah, it's very hard to say, with almost every show that actually makes it to Broadway there is a soundtrack album so it would be that and I can very easily visualize a soundtrack album that had the playbook bound into it but it's really too early to say.

Lilja: What else are you working on now? Is the new book taking up all your time or…

Stephen King: Yeah, it's basically the new book. I don't wanna talk about it because it always feels like bad luck to do that but it's a long book and it's set in Maine, not Florida, and I think that it's OK so far.

Lilja: In the past you have also written some scripts based on your books…

Stephen King: Yeah…

Lilja: Is that something you enjoy?

Stephen King: Sometimes… I wouldn't wanna say that I really enjoy it but I did a script for "The Gingerbread Girl" and that is in what I would call development hell right now. It's basically in the hands of Craig Baxley who directed *Storm of the Century* and *Rose Red* and Mark Carliner who produced *The Shining* miniseries and some of those other things and I would like to see that as a theatrical. I think it would make a good movie. Offers are out to various actors and actresses so now that the strike is over maybe something will happen or maybe nothing will happen. You just never know.

Lilja: Is it easier to write a script if you do it like with *Storm of the Century*, an original script or is it easier to base a script on a book?

Stephen King: I think originals are always easier and I think that scripts that are adapted are always easier when they are based on shorter works and I think those actually turn out a little bit better. I think that both *The Mist* and *1408* from last year are really good movies and both are based on shorter works. When you get a long book it's kinda like trying to stuff everything into a suitcase and that can be very difficult. *Duma Key* has been optioned for movies and it may actually become a movie but I was surprised that it happened because it's a story that has so much plot in it, it would really have to be simplified. *Lisey's Story* on the other hand would make a great TV miniseries if it was done in the right way.

Lilja: Yeah.

Stephen King: What are you watching now?

Lilja: I'm actually watching *LOST*. We're a couple of episodes behind you but that's an interesting show.

Stephen King: Yeah, it is. It's interesting, it's an interesting show, has interesting format and… yeah, it's good.

Lilja: It's going to be very interesting to see how they will tie it all up in the end.

Stephen King: You know what? I think they will actually be able to.

Lilja: Yeah? I hope so.

Speaking about *The Mist*. I just saw it recently and I must say that it's a really good movie.

Stephen King: Yeah, I think it is.

Lilja: It really survived very well in the transformation from story to movie. What are your feelings about Frank's new ending?

Stephen King: I thought it was good. The ending was obviously gonna be controversial but he had to put an ending to it, the story really doesn't have an ending. Before it could become a movie it had to be tied up. He couldn't just leave them there on the road which is what I did. And he became more and more convinced that the ending should be what the ending was when he did it. And originally it looked like it was going to be a Paramount movie and that they were gonna make it for a big budget, you know like *I am Legend* money, like 80 million, 90 million dollars but they wanted Frank to change the ending before they would do that. And Frank tried a number of different things, God bless him…I mean there is nothing wrong with that guy's heart or his willingness to work with other people, and none of it really rang true, nothing really worked so eventually he did the deal with The Weinstein's for Dimension Films. And they said "yes we'll go ahead and do it your way but we'll only go in for like 17 million dollars" so they kinda shot it quick and dirty.

Lilja: Yeah, and I think that was good for this one.

Stephen King: Yeah, I think so too. One thing that is interesting is that when the DVD comes out, which is fairly soon now, there's going to be two versions. There'll be the version that was released in theatres and there'll be another one that will be in black and white.

Lilja: Yeah, that one should be interesting.

Stephen King: Yeah, that's kind of the way that he wanted to do it from the very beginning. That will be interesting.

Lilja: I just have one more question and then I'll let you go.

Stephen King: OK…

Lilja: What about *The Talisman 3*? Any news on that?

Stephen King: [laughs] You mean the third section?

Lilja: Yeah.

Stephen King: Well, I talk to Peter about it and the real problem isn't working with Peter because I love to work with Peter and we actually have a really good idea for this book and I'm sure it'll happen in time but right now what it would mean is backing off and rereading those first two books and getting kinda back into the groove a bit and that's the part that's kinda holding me back, that's daunting. That's a lot of story there to beat around with, to work around so…

Lilja: It's about the same as when you were doing the last three *Dark Tower* books; you had to read up on them…

Stephen King: That's exactly what I was thinking of, yeah…

Lilja: I hope it won't be too long though…

Stephen King: This was great, I'll talk to you again.

Lilja: Yeah, I hope we can do this again.

Stephen King: OK, take care.

Lilja: Bye.

Afterword: 40 Years with the King

I have been reading Stephen King for forty years.

I run two web pages about King since, respectively 27 and 25 years.

Before this one, I have published three books about Stephen King. One of them has by now been issued in sixteen languages and in 36 different editions.

I have met Stephen King three times.

I have been granted interviews with King two times, and mine is the only fan site that he has ever given interview time.

The above is the numbers version of my history with Stephen King. Perhaps it sounds like boasting, but in truth I am very grateful, and humble, for my long relationship with Stephen King and his stories. The first of his books I ever read was a Christmas present from my parents in 1983, when they felt that at thirteen I was old enough to read novels instead of comic books. I have no idea of why they felt that *Carrie* was an appropriate novel to start with, but regardless of their reasoning I will always be grateful to them for giving me that particular book.

Would I have kept reading King for forty years if he had only written horror stories? Probably, but perhaps I wouldn't have appreciated his many books as much as I do, since their variation is one of the great benefits they offer. Don't misunderstand me. I in no way want to dispute that King is a great horror writer, and I love novels like *'Salem's Lot*, *Cujo*, *Pet Sematary* and *It*. Rather I want to stress that King writes so much more than only horror. I want to convince those who have no taste for horror to still give King a chance, so that they can experience his wonderful stories. One way of putting it might be that I want to prevent people from missing out on one of life's great boons.

Stephen King has published close to 90 books. Ten of them are collections of stories, four are non-fiction and the remaining are novels. His books can be placed in many different genres, including crime fiction (the Bill Hodges trilogy: *Mr. Mercedes*, *Finders Keepers*, *End of Watch*, Scribner 2014, 2015, 2016), fantasy (*The Talisman*), science fiction (*The Tommyknockers*, Putnam 1987; *Under the Dome*, Scribner 2009), time travel (*11.22.63*, Scribner, 2011), tragedy (*The Green Mile*), romance (*Bag of Bones*), coming of age stories (*Hearts in Atlantis*, "The Body", in *Different Seasons*, Viking 1982), and so on. And of course he has written one of the great fantasy epics, which incorporates elements from all of these and still more literary categories: *The Dark Tower*.

So while it is not untrue to claim that Stephen King is a master of horror fiction, it definitely is unfair. He is much more than that. I'm willing to say that if you like to read at all, Stephen King will have written something you will like. And if you don't like him right now, that's only because you still haven't discovered the book he wrote for you.

Acknowledgements

I wish to thank those who made this book what it is. If not for them, the final result would clearly have been worse, if indeed there had been any book at all.

George Beahm, who inspired me to write it and pushed me to get going.

Louise Lavér, Jimmie Rudolfsson, Christian Sjöblom, Carina Holm, Vincent Chong and Vesela Proshkova, who read an early draft and gave me valuable comments, corrections and suggestions.

Anders Jakobson who read more than one early version and gave me a truly professional report on his findings.

My publisher, Ekström & Garay, and particularly Melker Garay who pushed me on and believed in my ability to hammer out a book about King.

John-Henri Holmberg who translated this book from Swedish to English and thereby created the foundation on which all other editions are based.

Last but not least I of course also want to thank Stephen King. Without him, this book would most certainly not exist.

Thank you all!